Decolonising *Oikoumene*

Reimagining Church as Event: Perspectives from the Margins
Series Editors: George Zachariah and Sudipta Singh

In these eleven volumes, a collective of Indian theologians envisions Church as an Event that happens in particular contexts in the life of the communities at the margins. They argue that in the life of the communities who experience on their bodies the violence and hegemony of dominant power relations, morality, and religious dogmas and practices, the church happens as countercultural experiences that disrupt the logic of the prevailing order. These experiences enable and empower them to affirm and celebrate their differences, knowledges and beauty even as they weave their liberation. Church as event is a call to rising to life, creating life-flourishing communities that live out the foretaste of the reign of God.

Titles in this Series

Church and Religious Diversity Joshua Samuel and Samuel Mall
Church and Gender Justice Aruna Gnanadason
Faith in the Age of Empire Y.T. Vinayaraj
Dalitekklesia: A Church from Below Raj Bharat Patta
Church and Climate Justice Vinod Wesley
Church and Disability Samuel George
Church and Diakonia in the Age of COVID-19 Mothy Varkey
Decolonising Oikoumene Gladson Jathanna
Church and Human Sexuality Arvind Theodore
With Many Voices: Liturgies in Context Viji Varghese Eapen (Ed.)
The Word becoming Flesh George Zachariah

Decolonising *Oikoumene*

Gladson Jathanna

ISPCK

a partnership
of churches
in mission

2020

Decolonising *Oikoumene* - jointly published by the Indian Society for Promoting Christian Knowledge (ISPCK), Post Box 1585, Kashmere Gate, Delhi-110006 and Council for World Mission, Singapore-338729.

© Author, 2020

ISBN: 978-93-88945-82-0

Kindle Edition: 978-93-88945-95-0

Cover Illustration Credit : Immanuel Paul Vivekanandh K

Laser typeset by
ISPCK, Post Box 1585, 1654, Madarsa Road, Kashmere Gate, Delhi-110006 • *Tel:* 23866323
e-mail: ashish@ispck.org.in • ella@ispck.org.in
website: www.ispck.org.in
Printed at Saurabh Printers, NOIDA.

DEDICATION

To the Karnataka Theological College,
a regional ecumenical seminary in Mangalore,
that challenged me to dare to celebrate the
ecumenical spirit of difference, dissent,
multiplicity and manyness even when it was a costly affair.

We *Are* Because We Don't *Have*

*Upolu Luma Vaai**

We don't *have* the spirit
We *are* spirit
We don't *have* land
We *are* the land
We don't *have* the ocean
We *are* the ocean
We don't *have* relationship
We *are* relationship
We don't *have* stories
We *are* the story
Rooted
Connected
Fixed yet fluid in bonds of
Being in *Are*ness
Born from the depths
Of *In*ness
I am 'in' the community
The community is
'In' me

I live
Because
We *are*
A chorus of
Inextricable relatedness
Breathing concords
Of differences
Savouring variations
Of unity

Have!
And perish in
A unison of loss
Uttered by
One-truth ideologies
Secured by
Systems of oneness
Are!

An all becoming source
Whose becoming
I become
A genesis of harmony
Visible
In the sleeps of the stones
In the breaths of the trees
In the dreams of animals
In the whispers of clouds

In the speeches of waves
In the walking of mountains
In the re-turns of flowers
In the rhythms of life and death

We *are*
Because
We don't *have*

* Upolu Luma Vaai, "We Are Because We Don't Have." In *The Relational Self: Decolonising Personhood* in the Pacific. Edited by Upolu Luma Vaai and Unaisi Nabobo-Baba (Suva, Fiji: USP & PTC, 2017): 283-284.

Contents

Acknowledgements

The idea of ecumenism is strongly ingrained in the spirit of collectivity and connectivity. This book is a manifestation of such an ecumenical spirit. The book is utterly dependent on a wide range of people, friends, scholars and ecumenical leaders whom I have been both closely and distantly connected with.

First and foremost, I am deeply grateful to the Council for World Mission, in particular to Dr. Sudipta Singh, Mission Secretary, Research and Capacity Development, for his gracious invitation to undertake this project within the CWM's important initiative DARE (Discernment and Radical Engagement). I am indebted to his trust in me and the encouragement and support that he extended to me throughout the process of writing this book.

My sincere and deepest thanks to my beloved teacher and mentor Dr. George Zachariah, the editor of the series *Reimagining Church as Event: Perspectives from the Margins* of which this book is a part. He not only pulled me into this project but also shared his wisdom, knowledge and resources without which this project would not have materialised. He played a significant role in giving this book a pleasant shape through his sharp editorial critiques, comments and corrections.

I also place on record my sincere thanks to the Pacific Theological College, its Principal Dr. Upolu Luma Vaai and my colleagues for the pleasant collegiality and support. A special word of thanks to Prof. Vaai for allowing me to use his powerful poem that sets the tone and spirit of this book. I thank Dr. Holger Szesnat for reading some parts of the manuscript and providing constructive comments which helped in sharpening my arguments and inputs.

This book would not have been completed without the support and solidarity of my dearly beloved life-partner Sherly Snehalatha. I am deeply thankful to her for her love, patience and companionship. A special word of thanks is due to my parents and siblings for their prayers and blessings. My sincere thanks to Samuel Abraham for his friendly and critical feedback on the manuscript.

This book is grounded in my experiential contention that our notion of *oikoumene* epitomises a number of inner contradictions. On the one hand, it claims to cherish and celebrate diversities of beliefs, opinions, practices, traditions and theologies; but on the other hand, it suppresses the voices of difference, dissent and nonconformity in the name of unity and oneness. However, as the history of ecumenism demonstrates evidently, such architecture of imperial domination midwifes a generation of nonconformists who dare to redeem *oikoumene* from such inner absurdities. Hence, this book demonstrates an earnest hope in a decolonised space of *oikoumene* that invites us to celebrate not only diversity, difference, multiplicity, and manyness but also dissent and nonconformity. Such hope is transpired by my ecumenical voyage which has been a journey filled with challenges, struggles, fear, frustration, open wounds, moral anger and trauma. In this journey, the Karnataka Theological College (KTC), a regional ecumenical seminary in India, played a significant role in shaping my ecumenical belief. My sincere thanks to the community in KTC.

Foreword

DISCERNMENT AND RADICAL ENGAGEMENT (DARE) is an initiative of the Council for World Mission (CWM) to enable faith communities to *clarify what it means to engage in* public witness to God's justice and peace in a corrupt and conflicted world.

> The mission of DARE is conceived as the coming together of (a) the *radical soul* of discernment and sense-making in theology and biblical criticism; (b) the yearnings for *signifying engagement* that rise out of the slums of modernism and the valleys of despair; and (c) the commitment to redemption songs that *inspire disturbance* at the hubs of power.

As part of the DARE initiative, each region of CWM is invited to prepare and share biblical and theological resources on current themes and issues being considered by CWM, drawing upon the experiences and resources from the region.

Interfaith Engagement, Ecumenism and Inclusive communities against dehumanising social categorisations are the themes for the book series undertaken by the South Asia region of CWM. The thrust is centred on **Reimagining Church as Event: Perspectives from the Margins**. It calls to the fore persons living in the margins and highlights their voice, their narratives and their passion for a rearrangement of life in communities, as we know it, and a commitment to rise to life and to break out from Babylon. These books are intended for the use of lay people, pastors and evangelists as well as for theological students and seminaries. The series offer stories and narratives, analyses, liturgical resources, biblical, theological and ethical reflections, and missional/praxis proposals.

Church is an event that happens at the margins of contemporary life. Church happens as an epiphanic event where the divine presence is manifested and experienced in the pathos, struggles, contestations and harmonies of everyday existence. Church happens in those spaces where we celebrate the presence of Jesus, the Christ, in the flourishing of life. Church happens when we are transformed by one another, and inspired and enabled to engage in the transformative politics of the reign of God. Church happens whenever and wherever spirit-filled communities reclaim their subversive moral agency and contest the logic and practices of domination and exclusion. Church happens when the community experiences the healing power of the wounded healer and join Jesus in this risk-taking mission, despite the wounds we bear. To reimagine Church requires courage and commitment to engage in the mission of nurturing and organising communities of resistance and healing. This book series is a humble attempt at exposing and encouraging this radical expression of Church.

I appreciate and thank all those who are associated with this series, the authors, the contributors, the publishers and the editors. I commend this book series in the hope and prayers that they will help the faith communities in South Asia, and beyond, to *discern God's presence in community and dare to engage* in ways that re-present the God of life in communities and in the public square, *Rising to Life: Living out the New Heaven and New Earth.*

Colin Cowan
General Secretary
Council for World Mission

Introduction

*Asir Ebenezer**

Over a decade ago, the National Council of Churches in India embarked on an exercise of reconfiguration. This exercise went on for several years with each reconfiguring it the way that suited it. Somewhere along this exercise the discussions also centred on the nature of the ecumenical council. Some called it a united ecumenical expression; some an apex body of churches, ecumenical agencies and Christian organisations; and some others the ecumenical voice in India. None of these went without the required critique. Some among the members of the council thought it fit to define the council functionally rather than structurally. They came up with images of the household, which was not accepted since the biblical imagery of a household was patriarchal and hierarchical also with the open sanction of the practice of slavery. The imagery of a national platform was also not accepted since it is set up by some on which some others perform.

After all these discussions the imagery of a garden was acceptable to all, where there is place for all to flourish variedly in their own way, nurturing and complementing each other.

It needs to be mentioned here that this is much before the Commission on World Mission and Evangelism of the World Council of Churches embarked on the idea of associating mission with landscape, and hence indigenous to the land. Travelling further, the ecumenical discourses in India defined itself as a space where we do together what we otherwise could not do individually by ourselves. A very important example of this is the discourse on human sexuality which finds its location in this space—the National Ecumenical Forum for Gender and Sexual Diversities (NEFGSD) of the National Council of Churches in India. Attempts like these in different countries have tried to work around being the council of and established by churches and organisations, and moving towards practising ecumenism as structures, space and mission.

'Decolonising ecumenism' in the Discernment and Radical Engagement (DARE) series of the Council for World Mission (CWM) comes out as an academic work proposing to capture such indigenous articulations of ecumenical expressions everywhere and particularly outside the confines of ecumenism defined and practised in Western, European and World Christianity. The publication grows through an appraisal of ecumenism as a colonial project that which it was, to reimagining it in the form of ecumenism that is explicitly defined and manifested in manyness and multiplicity, and that which captures the mission of the multitudes in de-territorialised contexts.

The members of the CWM have given to themselves a new decade-long strategic plan. Flourishing life amidst a failing Babylon is the foundational theological basis for the plan. In the formulation of the foundational theological bases and locating them in Babylon *vis-à-vis* the hitherto location of the political or its northern economic allies, the CWM recognises that the empires located everywhere and in specific contexts have to be identified and, more importantly, named to be challenged locally and ecumenically. Coming as it were at this juncture, 'Decolonising ecumenism' will be a certain help to local churches in finding themselves growing as missional congregations indigenously and with an ecumenical spirituality. Reimagining Church as Event: Perspectives from the Margins within which this exercise is built provides a perfect opportunity therefore to live out the church locally and in fellowship with people of all faiths and beliefs.

At the turn of the century, the South Asian ecumenical landscape saw experiments as the South Asia Ecumenical Partnership Programme in which ecumenical councils, churches and their peers in different religions exercised that life is manifested in the coming together of two or three with a missional mandate for life flourishing (also of Jesus the Christ). Ecumenism in that phase of its historical narrative goes beyond structure and space, and the Jesus event in history thus becomes a mere pedagogical instrument to facilitate and/or acknowledge and recognise Christ events in every time and age and amidst all peoples and the *oikoumene*. This defies the logic of setting history in linear terms rather as from everywhere to everywhere redefining margins as centres with a multiplicity of multilaterally connected ecosystems.

Ecumenical spaces like the National Councils of Churches and similar regional and global configurations continue to be colonised by structures of church and Christian organisations. At times resource agencies with back donor baggage attempt to set or unsettle agendas. It is heartening to note that confessional bodies such as the Lutheran World Federation, the World Communion of Reformed Churches and global mission bodies such as the Council for World Mission take upon themselves the task of challenging their constituencies and in turn contributing to enriching their informed ecumenical engagements locally and in national, regional and global spaces.

Experiments in some Asian locations at least as represented in Korea, the Philippines, Indonesia and Taiwan seize their contexts of ecumenical engagements as the starting point of the discourse with no reference to existing traditional locations and frameworks that are anyway alien to their contexts and ethos. Through this lens we can take it that the present publication has taken upon itself the task of that exegesis of the past, which in most contexts are similar due to a seemingly common heritage of imperial context, both political and economic, providing the reader with the liberty to plunge deep into their own spaces to look for, document, research and develop indigenous and unique forms of ecumenical expressions and engagements. When this is done, ecumenical discourses of the dominant stand stripped of its colonial legacies and neocolonial hangovers paving the way for concerted and contextual life-flourishing engagements, which can interact and dialogue with similar contexts to cast an ecumenical national, regional and global collage of indigenous contextual concerted life flourishing and oikocentric engagements—a new decolonised ecumenical dawn.

* **The Rev. Asir Ebenezer** serves the National Council of Churches in India as General Secretary.

Prologue

At the beginning of the twenty-first century, Konrad Raiser, the former General Secretary of the World Council of Churches (WCC), stated with an anxious tenor about the future of ecumenism:

> In most churches ecumenism no longer seems to have the quality of a vision which mobilizes people to transcend inherited traditions and to engage in acts of renewal. The younger generation which, in the early stages of the ecumenical movement, was its main protagonist is less and less attracted by the search for visible institutional forms of church unity and cooperation. While there is a genuine spiritual quest, the concern for "being church" cannot easily be communicated, particularly through the secular media. Simultaneously, church leaders defending the commitment to ecumenical fellowship find themselves confronted with conservative and fundamentalist positions that identify ecumenism with tendencies that relativize and weaken the foundations of culture and religion. For many even the term "ecumenism" provokes suspicion and rejection.[1]

What was that provoked the ecumenical leader to raise such a grave concern about the future of the ecumenical movement? Did he observe a dampening of ecumenical excitement of two generations? These lines reflect the insignia of the anxiety of *ecumenical winter* which was, in the later years, foretold by many.[2] Several people have observed that the 'mainstream'

Protestantism that had been a driving force of the ecumenical movement has declined precipitously in recent decades, hence the ecumenical movement has come to a halt.[3] Is Raiser's apprehension worth a consideration? Was he right in his analysis that the contemporary ecumenical movement lack the quality of vision to transcend inherited traditions and to engage in acts of renewal? What are those "conservative and fundamentalist" positions that he was bidding to problematise? Suspicion and rejection of ecumenism!—What do they refer to?

From Raiser's fretfulness of *ecumenical winter*, let us now turn to a stimulating conversation between the current General Secretary of WCC, Olav Fykse Tveit, and Pope Benedict XVI in the autumn of 2010. The Norwegian Lutheran presbyter, while presenting a pair of Nordic woollen gloves to his Roman Catholic counterpart, the Pontiff, made this 'friendly' note:

> They say we are experiencing an 'ecumenical winter' right now. And I, being Norwegian, ask back, 'What is so terrible about winter?' We know that winter can be beautiful, and we know that winter is only one of four seasons. In winter, we have time for reflection, time to think about what we have experienced in the past and what we expect from the future, and, of course, how we can prepare for the future.[4]

It was indeed an insightful thought that looked at the possible *ecumenical winter* through optimistic and constructive lens. Moreover, Tveit roots his reflections conclusively in his own European context of 'beautiful' snowy-cold-winter and thus tries to embrace winter. But what does it mean to a person located in a tropical region, in the Pacific, and was born and brought up in another tropical region, the southwest of India, where winter can hardly be thought of as a metaphor of beauty? Though this book alludes to Tveit's approach, and agrees with his critique of the *ecumenical winter cliché*, it takes a somewhat different approach in conversing with the history of ecumenical movement particularly in Asia, and also in bringing in a few examples from the Pacific.

The book does not believe that ecumenism, especially, in Asia and the Pacific, is a halted or 'wintered' phenomenon. Rather, it affirms that ecumenism in these regions has the ability to share the sunshine with the rest of World Christianity. The major contention of the book is that the ecumenical movement in Asia and the Pacific has been a part of the larger decolonisation movement in the regions. Hence, a postcolonial methodological framework is taken as the guiding tool in this work.

The first chapter of the book wrestles with the definitions and concepts of *oikoumene* and problematises them from a postcolonial perspective. The second chapter takes up a significant ecumenical project, the World Missionary Conference, or the Edinburgh Missionary Conference, 1910 (Edinburgh 1910), as a case study to demonstrate the colonial captivity of the early ecumenical visions and missions. The third chapter is about ecumenism in Asia and the Pacific, highlighting the decolonising elements within those ecumenical discourses. Redefining *oikoumene* is the task of the fourth chapter, in which some glimpses of a radical vision for the future of ecumenism is shared. The book ends with three biblical reflections and two ecumenical liturgies to serve as a resource for further engagements with the ecumenical discourses.

The book is a project of the Council for World Mission's unique venture DARE (Discernment and Radical Engagement) in a Series on Reimagining Church as Event: Perspectives from the Margins. Hence, the perspectives shared in this book are obviously radical and rooted in the margins.

Endnotes

[1] "Report of the General Secretary," Ecumenical Review 54:4 (October 2002), 501–2

[2] See for example, Melanie Duguid-May, "The Ecumenical Movement," in History of Global Christianity, Volume III, History of Christianity in the 20th Century, edited by Jens Holger Schjorring, Norman A. Hjelm and Kevin Ward, Leiden, Boston: Brill, 2016: 147-181.

[3] Michael Root has observed in 2018 that the ecumenical movement has stopped moving. See Michael Root, "Ecumenical Winter": http://www.firstthings.com/article/2018/10/ecumenicalwinter

[4] "ÖRK-Chef: „Wir leben im ökumenischen Winter" Radio Vatican. 5 Dec. 2010. Transcript of radio interview, translated by Christian Schreiner. As Cited in Bruce Myers, "Keeping Warm. Reception in the Ecumenical Winter," The Ecumenical Review 65/3 (October 2013): 376-387; here 376.

CHAPTER 1

Oikoumene
Definitions and Problems

Introduction

This chapter looks critically at the term, definition and concept of *oikoumene*. It addresses the historical shift in understanding the idea of *oikoumene* specially focusing on the imperial notion of the term and concept, both in the Roman Empire and in Christendom. How did Christianity borrow and adopt the Roman idea of *oikoumene*? How did such an imperial idea legitimise the Western colonial project? Attempting to answer these questions, the present chapter explores and opens up a critical debate on the discourse surrounding *oikoumene*.

Oikoumene as a Democratic Vision?

Etymologically, the term ECUMENISM finds its root in the Greek word o*ikoumene*. A plain translation of the Greek word *oikoumene* would be "world" or "house." However, if we ask what notion did the Greek usage of the term had, the answer would be a little elaborated: *oikoumene* is the feminine passive participle of the verb *oikein*, which means *to dwell* or *to inhabit*.

Therefore, it would mean, "the whole inhabited world," or "a house that includes the whole inhabited world." The English word *ecumenical* comes from the adjective *oikoumenikos* pertaining to the whole world. This application of meaning had been viewed in the ecclesial context as quite a liberative and progressive aspect of Christian life. The World Council of Churches, having *Oikoumene* as the overarching slogan in its logo, attempts to reflect this meaning by its involvement in various liberation movements. As Konrad Raiser shows, the application of such a liberationist meaning came as a historical paradigmatic shift in the understanding of the concept *oikoumene* within the history of the ecumenical movement.[1] Hence, Raiser's paradigmatic shift indicates a calling to deinstitutionalise and de-dogmatise ecumenical processes.[2] Raiser assigns the ecumenical task to everyone applying the following convention: the householder (oikonomos) is to take care (oikonomia) of the life of all the household's (oikos) members.[3]

When Western Christian missions realised the urgency and inevitability of coming together for a collaborated venture in the mission field for a 'better success,' they ventured into the mission of ecumenism. In its initial years this word had become the sign of the unity of whole Christendom. *Oikoumene*, being the key word in the history of ecumenical movement, epitomises Christian unity as the prime and predominant ecumenical focus. In the course of its history the meaning and implication of the word *oikoumene* evolved from an exclusive understanding of Christian unity to the unity of whole community of creation, grounded on a democratic vision. However, in the history of Christianity, such *a democratic vision* of *oikoumene* was often troubled, contested and sometimes even disappeared. At the same time, *a colonial and imperial mission* of *oikoumene* was visibly evident throughout history.

Oikoumene **as a Colonial Mission?**

Barbara Rossing, in her excellent article "(Re)claiming *Oikoumene?*: Empire, Ecumenism, and the Discipleship of Equals," brings the historical fact that "by the first century BCE Rome laid claim to the *Oikoumene*."[4] She shows how in the expedition of Rome's conquests of lands and peoples, *oikoumene* was claimed not only to the ends of the world in a geographical sense but also in a political sense, as the ends of Roman imperial sway. Bringing in Claude Nicolet's findings that Rome's empire and its geographical knowledge developed hand in hand, she shows that an imperial project was evidenced in the use of the Greek word *oikoumene* and the Latin term *orbis terrarium*.[5] Nicolet finds that in the works of Greek historian Polybius (150 BCE), the geographical claims about the *oikoumene* were essentially political. He quotes Polybius: "All the known parts of the *oikoumene* have come under the domination of Rome."[6]

Rossing argues that Romans were called "lords of the *oikoumene*" *(kyrioi tes oikoumenes)*.[7] She brings in the examples of a trophy of the conquered *oikoumene* in 61 BCE, which was carried in triumphal procession in Rome to celebrate Pompey's three military victories over Libya, Europe and Asia. She cites from Dio's *Roman History*: "He [Pompey] celebrated the triumph in honor of all his wars at once, including in it many trophies beautifully decked out to represent each of his achievements, even the smallest; and after them all came one huge one, decked out in costly fashion and bearing an inscription stating that it was a trophy of the inhabited world [*oikoumene*]" (Dio, *Roman History* 37.21.2).[8] She brings in several examples of such kind from Julius Caesar, Augustus and other Roman emperors treading with their foot upon the *oikoumene*. All these examples of the use of the term *oikoumene* in the Roman Empire reflects imperial perspectives and its association with the empire.

These historical facts and examples make it clear that in the Roman times, the word *oikoumene* was used as a synonym for the Roman Empire. The Roman world being the *oikoumene* was seen as a civilised world whereas the colonised lands and people were seen as the 'uncivilised.' Pablo Richard, a Chilean scholar, makes this political reading of *oikoumene* as Rome: "The inhabited world, or *oikoumene*, is not all the earth, but the world that is organized and controlled by the Roman Empire. Everything else is the world of the barbarians."[9] Hence Rome saw *oikoumene*, its colonial 'mission', as a 'civilising' mission. K.M. George, an Indian Christian theologian, argues that the Roman Empire undertook this mission under the pretext of *Pax Romana* establishing a 'unity' within the empire by cutting through diversities.[10]

Christianity that grew in the context of the Roman Empire inherited the Roman imperial idea of *oikoumene* in its ecclesial life. It is quite evident in the history of Christianity that from the first ecumenical council of Nicaea, Christianity consistently maintained religious legitimacy of the Empire. These ecumenical councils that were convened by the Roman emperors established religious hegemony of the empire at that time. Christian faith was legitimised by the Roman Empire in those 'ecumenical councils' as an obligatory state religion to express loyalty to the empire. And moreover, these councils were called as *ecumenical* within the given dominant imperial definition of *oikoumene*. For example, as Robert Grant rightly points out, "The council of Nicaea was ecumenical only in the sense that the participants came from the Roman world...."[11] It was very evident that the early ecumenical councils created an undeniable link between the church's use of the word *ecumenical* and Rome's claims over the *oikoumene*. Jaroslav Pelikan explains this link clearly when he says, "That extension of the 'apostolic council' to a position of universal authority created the concept of the 'ecumenical council,' with 'ecumenical' here taking the double meaning of 'for the general church as a whole' and 'imperial in scope and in authority'...."[12] Hence, the early ecumenical councils were undoubtedly the products of the empire.

The modern colonial rhetoric and technologies reflect such an imperial idea of *oikoumene* in the Western colonisation of the non-West under the pretext of 'civilising' mission. The Western Christian missionary flow to the non-Western world benefited the colonial *ecumenical* project of the Western empires. With an integral association with the Western military forces, Christianity spread the idea of *oikoumene* in Asia, Latin America, Africa and the Pacific by the colonial project called *conversion* to 'one' belief system. Such a colonial project was legitimised by an imperial idea of the providence of God to 'civilise' the non-Western world. The Roman claims over the *oikoumene* was well reflected in those Western colonial conversion projects. Such notions could be found in the modern ecumenical movements as well. The next chapter seeks to demonstrate it by taking a much-celebrated ecumenical event, namely Edinburgh 1910, as a case study.

Conclusion

This brief chapter surveyed the meaning and implications of the idea of *oikoumene*. Highlighting the historical shift in understanding the idea of *oikoumene*, it is argued that the Roman imperial idea of *oikoumene* made its way to Christianity legitimising its colonial civilising mission projects. It is argued that the Roman claims over the *oikoumene* mirrored in the Western colonial conversion projects and also in the modern ecumenical movements. Therefore, the next chapter would analyse one such ecumenical project in order to identify the imperial impressions of *oikoumene* on the ecclesial life.

Endnotes

[1] Konrad Raiser, *Ecumenism in Transition*, Geneva: WCC, 1991.

[2] Marcin Lisak, "Socio-Religious Perspectives on the Ecumenical Paradigm Shift according to Konrad Raiser and Hans Kueng," *Angelicum* 93 (2016): 109-133; here, 118.

[3] Konrad Raiser, *Ecumenism in Transition*, 103-105.

[4] Barbara R. Rossing, "(Re)claiming *Oikoumene?*: Empire, Ecumenism, and the Discipleship of Equals," in *Walk in the Ways of Wisdom: Essays in Honor of Elisabeth Schuessler Fiorenza*, edited by Shelly Matthews et. al., Harrisburg, London, New York: Trinity Press International, 2003, 76.

[5] Claude Nicolet, *Space, Geography, and Politics in the Early Roman Empire*, Ann Arbor: University of Michigan Press, 1991, 11.

[6] Polybius, *Histories 3.1.4*. As cited by Nicolet, *Space, Geography, and Politics*, 30.

[7] Barbara R. Rossing, (Re)claiming *Oikoumene?*, 76.

[8] Barbara R. Rossing, (Re)claiming *Oikoumene?*, 76.

[9] Pablo Richard, *Apocalypse: A People's Commentary on the Book of Revelation*, Maryknoll, NY: Orbis, 1995, 61.

[10] K. M. George, "Values for New Ecumenism in Asia," in *Living in Oikoumene* edited by Hope S. Antone, Hong Kong: CCA, 2003, 78-87

[11] Robert M. Grant, Religion and Politics at the Council of Nicaea," *Journal of Religion*, Vol. 55, No. 1 (Jan., 1975): 1-12; here, 1.

[12] Jaroslav Pelikan, *The Excellent Empire: The Fall of Rome and the Triumph of the Church*, San Francisco: Harper & Row, 1987, 26.

CHAPTER 2

Revisiting Colonial Ecumenical Project (Edinburgh 1910 – A Case Study)

Introduction

As discussed in the previous chapter, the modern missionary influx in the colonial context was burdened by an expansionist notion of the *oikoumene*. William Carey (1761–1834), who is regarded as one of the architects of the modern missionary movement, was convinced that the "New Testament command to preach gospel to every creature was as binding upon the Christians of all times as it was upon the apostles."[1] His faith legitimised not only the expansion of Christianity but also its counterpart—colonialism. Gustav Warneck (1834–1910), who has been characterised as the "founder not only of the German missiology but also of that of the Protestants" and as the "educator of the church for mission," states: "I understand by missions the whole operation of Christendom directed towards the planting and organization of the Christian church among non-Christians."[2] These two voices from two different centuries in the modern time reflect very well the Roman notion of *oikoumene*. They also represent different faces of the two distinct theological positions, both having the imperial mission of establishing an *oikoumene*: one, an attempt to draw human beings out of a "sinful" world and to absorb them into the church, just as the Roman Empire attempted to 'redeem' the 'uncivilised' non-Roman world to the *oikoumene* of Rome; and the other, to accentuate the need for 'social transformation' and 'redemption of history' as a demand of Christian faith and commitment, similar to what the Roman Empire claimed as bringing 'social transformation' and 'redemption' through its colonial project *Pax Romana*. It is quite noteworthy that such an expansionist Roman-model ecumenical and missiological motif is so obvious in all the modern ecumenical discourses, including the much-celebrated Edinburgh 1910. Edinburgh 1910 was, indeed, a persistent reminder to all the European mission agencies to march towards this goal without bothering to listen to the alternative voices however genuine they might be.

Standing at the crossroads of the centenary of a well-celebrated World Missionary Conference and a globalised world economy, one has to be aware of the fact that the terms 'mission' always had a terrorising imperial connotation. M.P. Joseph rightly argues,

> Both in the military adventures and in the ecclesiastical usage, the term mission assumes the possession and ownership of an absolute knowledge of a normative which others are ought to follow. Modern missionary movements started with a claim of an absolute knowledge of God and an imposition of a single truth on a plural world. This claim of an exclusive knowledge of soteriology tends to rationalise a utilitarian principle. Destruction of the other is justified in the name of goodness and civilisation. Colonialism is one of the projects rationalised by this principle. Military brutalities of the recent times are not different. Mission

of the cluster bombs is to ensure self-determination and freedom to the very people who have been killed by the same bombs.[3]

History shows that all absolute claims are imperial projects, attempting to invade and interiorise the outside into their systems of living. Ecumenical projects are not exceptions.

Therefore, this chapter would attempt to revisit the modern ecumenical project, taking up the ecumenical conference of Edinburgh 1910 and its multiple discourses as case study. The major focus of the chapter is manifold: 1. To unearth how an imperial theology of *oikoumene* was quite inherent in the Edinburgh discourse; 2. To critically evaluate the colonial political implications of the ecumenical project; and 3. To highlight how the Western epistemological impositions on the non-West were challenged within the ecumenical discourses.

One Christ for All: An Imperial Theology of *Oikoumene*

The World Missionary Conference had its root in a Christianising, imperialising and colonising call by John R. Mott "to evangelize the world in this generation." Mott was convinced that this challenge "rests securely upon Divine commandment." He wrote: "The Great Commission of Christ given by Him in the Upper Room in Jerusalem on the night after the resurrection, again a little later on a mountain in Galilee, and yet again, on the Mount of Olives, just before the ascension clearly expresses our obligation to make Christ known to all men."[4] Such an interpretation was a very motivating tool for the missionaries of his time. It motivated mission organisations and churches in kindling the hope of experiencing the emergence of a unified world religious culture and practice informed by the gospel imperatives. This approach constructed, what M.P. Joseph calls, "a bi-polar world view." This view, as he rightly argues, "assumes the existence of two mutually exclusive worlds, the Christian world and the non-Christian world. This missionary geography proposes that human salvation is possible only within the ambit of the Christian world, and they do have a mandate to save those who are outside the Christian world from eternal doom."[5] With this conviction the creation of an *ecumenical* organisation representing all mission societies came into being.[6]

Among the various commission reports to that conference, the report of the first commission to the conference, "Carrying the Gospel to All the Non-Christian World," was considered "the most important commission of the conference."[7] The reports of these commissions are clear manifestations of the Western imperial notion of *oikoumene*, an imperial project of superimposing Western rationality on the non-Western world. A large number of the missionary enterprises had undertaken with zeal the promotion of a Western scientific rationality informed by the European Enlightenment. Such a campaign of the new rationality against the traditional wisdom of the non-Western world was conceived as a civilisational imperative and thus it was carried out with utmost earnestness. Furthermore, the new scientific rationality was presented as the only universal remedy for a lack of growth and prosperity. The best example for the influence of the Enlightenment agenda within the mission mandate was evident from the prominence attached to imparting 'secular education' and furtherance of institutional health-care systems at the expense of the primal medical systems of the people.

The Commission I report states that "some missionaries believe that prior to a vigorous campaign of evangelization what is most needed at the present time is to promote the work of educational missions."[8] It is through this Western education that the conference was pressing to make all the non-Christian world Christian. It quotes a Scottish missionary:

> [N]ow a days no bonafide idolater is to be found in the schools and universities managed by the Europeans. Their adherence to idolatrous ceremonies is either formal from fear of society, or is defended on the ground that such practices are a help to concentration of thought on religion.

These examples inform us that the vision of Christian ecumenism was a mere replica of the mission of the Roman Empire to legitimise one's superiority over the other. However, such imperial notions of *oikoumene* were severely resisted by the colonised. One such resisting voice was Pandita Ramabai, an Indian representative who writes in her letter to the Commission I:

> The majority of the higher classes are getting western secular education, which is undermining their faith in their ancestral religion. They are not getting anything better to take the place of the old religion in their hearts, and are therefore without God, without hope, without Christ, going down socially and morally, and becoming very irreligious.[9]

The report, however, laments: "With the influx of European civilization into Africa and Asia there seems to have come a flood of pernicious influences, of vice, and of disease."[10]

Oikoumene: A Political Justification for Christian Mission

The Edinburgh Conference was organised and carried out with the help of colonial monetarism and European patriotism. The Commission I report clearly states a political ground for the need and urgency of Christian mission:

> One of the most significant and hopeful facts with reference to world evangelization is that the vast majority of the people of the non-Christian nations and races are under the sway, either of Christian governments or of those not antagonistic to Christian

missions. This should greatly facilitate the carrying out of a comprehensive campaign to make Christ known.[11]

This becomes very clear when King George V of England and the Secretary of State of the imperial German Colonial Office sent greetings to the participants of the Edinburgh Conference. Former United States President Theodore Roosevelt was a prospective delegate but later sent a letter of regret for his absence. Generals of the colonial administrations were present throughout the conference, signifying the mutual importance of the mission agenda and the colonial project. In his greetings, King George V observed that the "dissemination of the knowledge and principles of Christianity by Christian methods throughout the world" would usher in the cause of "peace and the well-being of all." The conference responded positively and thanked the King for his political leadership as the emperor of the world.[12] This was the faith and conviction of the West that colonised many parts of the world.

The earlier Missionary Conference in 1900 observed that "the political and commercial expansion and occupation of distant land by Europe and America had directed the thoughts of Christendom to distant parts of the earth."[13] Three times the report recollects the so-called conversion story of Emperor Constantine and implies that conversion is a God-given 'mission' of the state. However, one should not forget that this story of so-called conversion[14] of Constantine has an imperial implication to the non-West. Rulers are always in search for a rational explanation for their hegemonic power. Unfortunately, history tells us that in most cases the rational legitimisation comes from the claim of their proximity to God!

The language of the conference makes it clear that the West is the maker of human history whereas the Other, the non-West, are mere voiceless receivers. Their convictions were: We, the Christians, have salvation and they, the non-Christians, have sin. We, the Westerners, have wealth and they, the Others, have poverty. We, the Europeans, have rational knowledge and they, the Orients, have irrational primitive knowledge. Thus it is the legitimate burden of the haves to give to the have-nots. The introductory statement which gives the rationale behind inviting more than 1,200 people to Edinburgh for the International Missionary Conference alluded to the unparalleled growth of resources in the Western hemisphere. It states the following:

> It is possible today as never before to have a campaign adequate to carry the Gospel to all the non-Christian world so far as the Christian Church is concerned. Its resources are more than adequate …. The money power in the hands of believing Christians of our generation is enormous.[15]

The findings of the commission were that "it is an opportune time"; "a combination of opportunities" awaits us among the "primitive and cultured" in the "world field"; so "open and accessible."[16]

Oikoumene: A Sociocultural Rationalisation of Binaries

Gayatri Spivak, highlighting possible theories for the study of cultural encounters, judges that one of the important contributions of French Poststructuralist theory is that the "intellectuals must attempt to disclose and know the discourse of society's Other."[17] By intellectuals, she meant all those who study or attempt to read the encounters between the Self and the Other. It is very clear that Edinburgh 1910 had constructed a strong 'Other' in its treatment of non-Christian beliefs and cultures of the world. This is very well reflected in the texts that are produced as a result of the conference. They stand as a major part of the European body of knowledge for studies such as cultural encounters, mission studies and social history.

These texts fall into the category of what Edward Said calls Orientalism. According to him, such a unified, international body of knowledge describes Orientals as being uncivilised, unprogressive, immoral, passive, emotional, sensual, and having an extensive list of other unsavoury characteristics. This body of knowledge is embodied in what Said calls a "discourse."[18] Said also acknowledges that European policies and actions towards the Orients are part of the Orientalist "discourse."[19] In line of his argument it could be argued that the reports of the Edinburgh Conference, being the texts of European knowledge, make a part of the Orientalist discourses. The Orients in these texts find a culturally inferior position. This attempt of pushing a particular culture into a positional inferiority needs to be disclosed to all.

The reports of different commissions of Edinburgh 1910 contain a strong dualistic nature of Orientalism, and this dualism makes hard and fast distinctions between the 'civilised' Western culture and the 'uncivilised' Eastern culture; the culture of 'scientific' knowledge and the culture of 'primitive' knowledge. A sturdy distinction is constructed between 'our' culture and the culture of 'others'; 'Us and Them,' and 'We and They.' It creates a notion that the European culture is progressive and dynamic whereas the Orients have an essentially stagnant and unchanging culture. They do not know themselves nearly as well as the Europeans know them.

Edinburgh 1910 has consistently divided the world into two antagonistic, incompatible realms of Christian and non-Christian. These writings frequently describe the non-Christian world as being immoral, benighted, idolatrous, pagan, barbaric, infidel, and so on. All these descriptions could be summed up in one word which is very frequently and commonly used in the reports of different commissions, especially Commission I and Commission IV, i.e. "heathenism."

The Edinburgh ecumenical discourse was aggressive and derogatory in its treatment of people of different living faiths, expressing attitudes that have frequently included negative views of Oriental religions and cultures. These reports include the voices of many missionaries who were presently living with the Orients—of course, with the 'burden' of Christian mission. Even though these missionaries visited the houses of the Orients, shared love and moved together, they seemed never quite to forget that those natives were representatives of a 'less advanced' and 'heathen' culture.[20] And they defined the people of different living faiths as "outsiders" who are damned to eternal punishment and suffering. It implies and reflects the dominance of the logic of oneness that guided the ecumenical discussions at the cost of demonising manyness celebrated in the 'mission fields.'

Conclusion

Colonialism, conversion and conquering through faith were at the heart of the ecumenical gathering in Edinburgh 1910 and they represented three major technologies of power. Such technologies of domination were not unquestioned by the *ecumenical other*, as the foundation for a new form of *ecumenicity*. But the written discourse of Edinburgh 1910 does not seem to care for such questionings. V.S. Azariah, one of the Indian representatives of the conference, intervened very powerfully in these words:

> The problem of race relationships is one of the most serious problems confronting the Church today. The bridging of the gulf between the East and the West, and the attainment of a greater unity and common ground in Christ as the great Unifier of mankind, is one of the deepest needs of our time.

Such interventions were the attempts of the non-West to a search for alternative forms of *oikoumene* that could rejoin spirituality and politics. It indicates that the non-Western participants of ecumenical gatherings believed that such new forms of *oikoumene* as an expression of spirituality could break norms and prevent the creation of hegemonic and homogenised societies through the act of making known one Jesus of Nazareth to the entire world. This voice of a church leader from India is still relevant in our contemporary context as we continue to grapple with the content and meaning of *oikoumene* in the context of globalisation and market economy, where the technologies of power dominate, rooted in their geographical and political location, space and time.

Endnotes

[1] William Carey, "An Enquiry into Obligations of the Christians to Use means for the Conversion of the heathen," in *Classics of Christian Missions*, edited by F. M. DuBose, Nashville: Broadman, 1979, 24.

[2] H. Kasdorf, *Gustav Warnecks Missiologisches Erbe. Eine Biographisch-historische Untersuchung*, Gießen und Basel: Brunnen Verlag, 1990, iii.

[3] M. P. Joseph, "Revisiting the Edinburgh Conference in the Context of Globalization," in *Witnessing in Context. Essays in Honor of Eardly Mendis*, edited by Monica J. Melanchthon and George Zachariah, Tiruvalla:CSS, 2007, 153.

[4] John R. Mott, "The Obligation to Evangelize the World," repr. in *Classics of Christian Missions*, edited by F. M. DuBose, Nashville: Broadman, 1979, 320f.

[5] M. P. Joseph, "Revisiting the Edinburgh Conference," 157.

[6] It has to be noted that much prior to Mott, William Carey proposed in 1806 that a general missionary conference should be held in 1810 in order to consolidate the missionary energy for a rapid geographical expansion of the work.

[7] Clements, *Faith on the Frontier*, 80.

[8] World Missionary Conference 1910, *Carrying the Gospel to All the Non-Christian World*, Edinburgh and London, 1910, 9.

9 World Missionary Conference 1910, 30f.

10 World Missionary Conference 1910, 22.

11 World Missionary Conference 1910, 6.

12 H. Sawyerr, "The First World Missionary Conference. Edinburgh 1910," *International Review of Mission*, LXVII (1978): 255–272; here, 267.

13 Ecumenical Missionary Conference 1900, *Report*, Vol. 1, New York: American Tract Society, 1900, 10.

14 It is important to note, at least as a cross reference, the works of several scholars who critically look into the legitimacy and historicity of Eusebius' narratives of the 'conversion' of Constantine. Many have argued that the narrative legitimises Constantine's political allegiance to the god of battles and hence gives a legitimate sanction to his wars and invasions. See, Diarmaid MacCulloch, *Christianity. The First Three Thousand Years*, New York:Viking, 2009: Chapter 6; Wes Howard-Brook, *Empire Baptized. How the Church Embraced What Jesus Rejected (Second-Fifth Centuries)*, Maryknoll, New York: Orbis Books, 2016: 191-198; Justo L. Gonzales, *The Story of Christianity* Vol.1, New York: HarperOne, 2010: Chapter 13.

15 World Missionary Conference, *Carrying the Gospel*, 10.

16 Ibid.

17 Gayatri C. Spivak, "Can the Subaltern Speak?," in *Postcolonialism. Critical Concepts*, edited by D. Brydon, Vol. IV, London and New York: Routledge, 2000, 1427–1477.

18 Edward Said, *Orientalism*, London: Pantheon Books 1978, Reprint: 1995, 73.

19 Ibid., 73.

20 Jacob S. Dharmaraj, *Colonialism and Christian Mission. Postcolonial Reflections*, Delhi: ISPCK, 1993, 42.

CHAPTER 3

Decolonising *Oikoumene*
A Postcolonial Project

Introduction

While the previous chapter, taking a Eurocentric ecumenical gathering as a case study, demonstrated that the ecumenical movement in the predominant part of the twentieth century had the colonial burden of *uniting* Christendom, this chapter exhibits how marginal locations such as Asia and the Pacific subverted the colonial implications of ecumenism and used them as a potential tool in their movements towards decolonisation. This chapter engages with the efforts of Asian and Oceanic Christianity that deterritorialised ecumenism by challenging the Western impositions and claiming distinct entries to the perception of ecumenism. It also converses with a few selected theological voices from the margins and exhibits how they decolonised the dominant Eurocentric ecumenical theologies and re-envisioned distinct ecumenical theologies that are contextually rooted and politically articulated. Looking at the role of Asian women, students and youth in the ecumenical movement, the chapter identifies some major contributions made by Asian women, students and youth towards decolonising *oikoumene*. At the end, it briefly discusses the wider question of ecumenism in multifaith contexts, taking examples from the history of Asian ecumenism.

Deterritorialising Ecumenism: A Marginal Intervention

It is argued very often and very commonly that modern ecumenism is the child of Western missionary movement. Even the non-West is made to believe and internalise such colonial claim.[1] However, contrary to such claims, already in 1994 Indian church historian T. V. Philip had challenged this Eurocentric historicism. He says:

> Western historians cite as evidence for their argument that the missionary conferences in mission fields and in the West led to the great World Missionary Conference in 1910 at Edinburgh, which is considered to be the beginning of the modern ecumenical movement. It must be noted that the missionary conferences in mission fields were concerned with cooperation in mission for the sake of evangelistic efficiency, but not with unity as such. The real impetus for Christian unity came from Asian Christians, who under the inspiration of the national movement took the initiative for Christian unity and for the building up of indigenous churches. In fact, it was the protest of the Asian Christians against Western denominationalism and missionary paternalism which led to church unity discussions in some of the missionary conferences. The Asians not only initiated ecumenical ventures in Asia, but also contributed, through the missionary movement, to the ecumenical developments in the West.[2]

The crux of the matter here is that the modern ecumenical movement was a part of the process of decolonisation in the Global South.[3] The spirit of nationalism in the erstwhile colonised territories had a great impact on the way the church thought and perceived her mission and vision. Indigenous leaders in different parts of the Global South understood that the mission of the church was to liberate herself from the colonialisation of the West. As Philip rightly claims, the ecumenical movement in Asia, which was inspired by the nationalist movements, was part of the liberation/freedom movements in Asia. Such liberation movements demanded not only redemption from ecclesiastical colonialism but also a holistic redemption towards building independent nations in the Global South.

The well-celebrated ecumenical gathering at Edinburgh in 1910 witnessed the strong sign of such liberation movements. As Kim Caroline Sanecki demonstrates, the presence of the so-called younger churches from non-Western lands challenged the silence or support of the Western missionary agencies towards Western colonialism.[4] Even the World Missionary Conference of Edinburgh 1910, which is said to be the first international 'ecumenical' gathering, was aware of such strong interrogations from the Global South. The following reference to the Report of the Commission I, for example, stands as an exemplary evidence for this:

> There is a widespread movement among the nations and people of Asia, Africa, and Oceania toward independence of European and American control and influence.... This national movement in almost every place is the expression of the growing self-consciousness of the peoples. They are proud of their past; they believe they have resources and ability to make their own contribution to the life of the world. They wish to preserve their individuality and independence, and to develop and be true to their national and racial characteristics.[5]

The Commission also affirmed that,

> [T]his national and racial spirit cannot and should not be crushed or checked. It is a matter of profound concern to the Christian Church. It will have much power to hinder or to facilitate the spread of Christ's Kingdom. Christ never by teaching or example resisted or withstood the spirit of true nationalism.[6]

On the other hand, significant ecumenical personalities like John R. Mott had already started to advocate that the deep sense of anti-colonial patriotism rising in the Global South was a potential 'difficulty' for Western Christianity to extend its mission of evangelism. As he wrote in his famous book, *The Evangelization of the World in this Generation*, ten years prior to the World Missionary Conference in Edinburgh,

> Another difficulty, in a sense political, is the national feeling found in Japan, which regards the acceptance of Christianity as disloyalty to the Emperor. In India also there is *a false patriotism* [emphasis mine] which identifies love of country with firm adherence to the ancient faith.[7]

It is interesting to note that Mott places two different 'nationalism' discourses parallel to each other without bothering to care for their differences and distinctivities. His observation on Indian nationalism, when read in the face of contemporary rule of fascist government in India, holds much value. But the context he was referring to base his allegation against Indian nationalism was a British imperial context, where Indian 'firm adherence to the ancient faith,' had much to do with self-determination against a foreign rule. However, in a contrast line of certainty, the ecumenical gathering believed that,

> [T]he development and spread of the spirit of national and racial patriotism constitutes a most inspiring summons to carry the Gospel of Christ to all these peoples. Pure Christianity should be brought to bear at once in order to help to educate, purify, unify, guide, and strengthen the national spirit.[8]

Undisputedly, that was the Orientalist and colonial spirit of 'modern' ecumenism. It saw the national spirit and the movement towards independence and liberation in the non-Western world as an *opportunity* to spread the Eurocentric spirituality and Western colonial superiority in the non-Western world.

It also displays how the early ecumenical gatherings skilfully abstained from openly condemning the empires. While some ecumenical personalities were critical about the ill effects of imperialism when it interfered with missionary work, no one openly questioned it.[9]

On the other hand, Christians from different parts of the Global South were constantly challenging such Eurocentric and Orientalist worldview of the modern ecumenical gathering. Cheng Ching-yi, one among the only seventeen Asian missionary leaders in the World Missionary Conference in Edinburgh, reminded his Western counterparts with his sharp words: "...But friends, do not forget to view us from our standpoint, and if you fail to do that, the Chinese will remain always as a mysterious people to you!"[10] It was the Orientalist and colonial gaze of the Western 'ecumenical' partners and their racial superiority that the ecumenical representative from China was challenging. Likewise, it is worth remembering the Indian delegate Bishop Azariah's categorical reminder to his international audience at the conference: "The problem of race relationship is one of the most serious problems confronting the Church to-day."[11]

The spirit of deterritorialising Christianity in the Global South always formed one of the cores of ecumenical life force. The continuous demand for autonomy was always echoed in the ecumenical gatherings. The delegates from East Asia, especially from the Chinese and Indian national councils, in the International Missionary Council in Tambaram, India, in 1938, demanded an independent Asian regional ecumenical committee.[12] It was not just an Asian call to establish a regional ecumenical office, rather it was a deliberate demand to deterritorialise Eurocentred ecumenical framework. As a response, the East Asia Christian Conference (the present

Christian Conference of Asia) came into being in 1957 in Parapat, Indonesia. As Wati Longchar opines, "[T]he churches in Asia came together in Parapat with the conviction that dissection of the body of Christ is a scandal of faith and imperialism is contrary to the teaching of our Lord Jesus Christ."[13] Hence, the Christian Conference of Asia was essentially a non-Western ecumenical entity independent from the paternalism and domination of Western Christianity. As M. M. Thomas has rightly observed, the ecumenical gathering at Tambaram reflected "the new search by Asian churches for their selfhood freed from the paternalism and domination of missions to be able to relate themselves to the emerging national selfhood of their peoples within the universality of the worldwide church."[14]

The formation of the Church of South India, and the following similar Church unions in north India, Sri Lanka, Pakistan, and elsewhere, was another evidential landmark in the journey of the churches in the Global South that sought to redefine *oikoumene* as a deterritorialising movement. As historian George Oommen rightly points out, "[I]n its formation, the Church of South India sought to break through Western patterns of denominationalism, seeing itself not as just one more church body, but as a means toward bringing together other churches."[15] When the Mar Thoma Church entered into conciliar unity with the Church of South India and the Church of North India to form the Communion of Churches in India (CCI),[16] the movement of deterritorialisation found a greater impetus. As Jesudas Athyal points out, "In the formation of the Churches of South and North India and the Church of Pakistan when denominational differences were resolved within one organic unity, and later in the coming together of three churches in the CCI in conciliar unity, South Asia demonstrated the possibility for diverse and indigenous forms of unity and witness that transcend established Western paradigms."[17] This challenged the denominationally territorialised Christianity of the West and claimed a distinct ecumenical spirit that defined unity not fully in terms of the understanding of the Western churches, but in terms of local understanding that was rooted in local and regional epistemologies and experiences.

Moreover, the idea of *local ecumenism* came out intensely through the regional councils of churches. The regional councils played significant roles in supporting localised ecclesial expressions. As the third assembly of the WCC in New Delhi captured the spirit of the time, which dreamed of and celebrated *local ecumenism,* in its statement on unity, "[T]he place where the development of the common life in Christ is most clearly tested is in the local situation, where believers live and work."[18] The regional councils, especially in the Global South such as Asia (1959), Africa (1963), the Pacific (1966), Caribbean (1973), the Middle East (1974) and Latin America (1982), often challenged the Eurocentric style of working of the World Council of Churches. Though the fourth general assembly in Uppsala created a secretariat "to give continuous attention to the development of relationships of mutual helpfulness between the WCC and national council of churches (NCCs) and other Christian councils,"[19] it did not help much. The local ecumenical councils challenged the World Council's regional activities and even its direct relationship with member churches. And in the seventh general assembly in Canberra in 1991, a "Guiding Principles for Relationships and Cooperation between the Regional Ecumenical Organization and the World Council of Churches"[20] was established in order to establish a healthy cooperation between the *local* ecumenical bodies and the *international* ecumenical office.

However, the *local* in the Global South, which is distinctly diverse and heterogeneous in its multicultural, multireligious and multi-ethnic realities, is a complex category. The *local* is often defined within imperial categories and structures. For example, the spirit of nationalism that drew the churches in the Global South to the urgency of redefining ecumenism was often an elite nationalism. Marginal communities such as indigenous people, Dalits, Tribals, women and so on were always placed outside the *local* epistemologies of the nationalistic spirit.[21] It was the liberation theologies in the Global South that gave a new impetus to the ecumenical movement striving to redefine the *local* by bringing in the marginal voices into ecumenical discourses. The Christian Conference of Asia, when it met in Bangkok in 1968, "emphasized the significance of Asian people's movements and struggle for justice and freedom and asked the churches to stand ready to endorse the responsible use of civil disobedience in cases where law and distribution of power were unjust."[22] The *regional* ecumenical movement in the Global South started to respond to military imperialism and tabled the plight of the marginalised as communities and people for genuine intervention as an important and integral part of ecumenical spirituality.

At the same time, it was not always *local ecumenism* at the Global South verses *Western ecumenism*. Korean ecumenical narratives, for example, tell us a different story altogether. As it is argued above, the history of ecumenical movement in Asia was very much associated with Western imperialism. But that was not all. There has been also internal colonialism and imperialism. The Korean national sovereignty, for example, was not threatened by any Western power, but by Japan, an Asian empire. As Ahn Kyo-Seong observes,

> The Japanese empire were eager for putting Christianity, including the ecumenical movement, under control. In the beginning of colonial rule, Japan attempted to domesticate them, on the one hand, and offered them carrot, on the other. Towards the end of colonial rule, however, Japan forged a union church by consolidating denominations and abolished the interdenominational ecumenical body called the Korean National Christian Council .... Such forced merger and abolition were applied both in metropolitan Japan and colonial Korea.[23]

What is highly important here to note is the fact that in the distinct Asian context, ecumenism posed the challenge to move from regional/local imperial ecumenism to regional/local nationalistic ecumenism.

Let me bring in a rather recent example from a different part of the Global South—the Pacific or Oceania. In 2017, the Pacific Church Leaders Meeting took place in Auckland, New Zealand, to review and revitalise the journey of ecumenical movement in the Pacific. The meeting held that no longer would ecumenism in the Pacific mean "Unity of the Body of Christ" but the "Household of God in the Pacific."[24] This indeed deterritorialised the definition of ecumenism from the European and the North American churches' territorial definition, grounded on their Eurocentric worldview. In the 11th General Assembly of the Pacific Conference of Churches in the following year, Tevita Havea, in his address as Moderator, made this profound statement:

> We must script the new story of our ecumenical journey together; it cannot be otherwise. This is our task, not someone else's.

Today, our mission stories ought to focus on dismantling today's dominant single story of the 'good life' which says that our sole purpose in life is economic productivity and consumption.[25]

Deterritorialising ecumenism in the Oceania, though Havea calls it "scripting the new story...dismantling *today's* dominant single story...," was not a new phenomenon of the twenty-first century. Right from the beginning of its organised ecumenical voyage, Christianity in the Oceanic Islands has been consciously attempting to redefine ecumenism in its own distinctive Oceanic terms and vocabularies strongly based in the colonial and postcolonial Oceanic context. As Fele Nokise, a church historian in the Pacific, observes, "Our hermeneutical experience of ecumenism and since 1961 has been on the main, a relentless journey of discovery and re-discovery into non-chartered territory."[26] The Churches in the Pacific identify 1961[27] as the beginning of an organised ecumenical journey, with the first meeting of Pacific Churches being held at Malua in Samoa in that year. The sociopolitical matrix of Oceania during that time, which was defined and shaped by strong anti-colonial movement and the fight for freedom, set the framework for discerning and appropriating the spirit of ecumenism in the Oceanic context. As Nokise observes, "The attainment by Samoa of independence status in 1962 had a domino effect on other island countries who were trying to shake off the shackles of colonialism."[28]

The Pacific Conference of Churches (PCC), which came into being in 1962 as an ecumenical body of the Pacific churches, affirmed the urgent need for "Rethinking the Household of God."[29] This affirmation called for "the churches to strive toward greater solidarity, inclusiveness and participation around issues of concern to the people of the Pacific. The key aspects of this endeavour relate to development, peace and security, governance and leadership, climate change and resettlement, and cultural and social cohesion."[30] Historians and ecumenical scholars in the Pacific rightly observe that the PCC's origin was a response to the decolonisation process that was happening worldwide at that time. They argue that the initial ecumenical enthusiasm in the Pacific was strongly connected to the recent formation of the WCC and the worldwide movement for political decolonisation and self-determination.[31]

In the 1960s and 1970s most island nations in the Pacific obtained political independence. Such decolonisation also resulted in the urge for independent thinking, self-determination, greater cultural consciousness, and increasing economic regionalism. As an offshoot of decolonisation, the Pacific Theological College, an ecumenical theological college for the Protestant Churches in the Pacific, came into being in 1965, and the Pacific Regional Seminary, for the Catholic Church, in 1972. As the Pacific delegation at the ecumenical gathering of the 'Third World' rightly identified, the Pacific theologians became more exposed to indigenous and contextual theologies with the growing realisation that theology "is the human response in faith to the living God that can never be contained in any one tradition of human responses."[32] As Anna Anisi and Aisake Casimira argue, "[T]his awakening process that was happening within the churches was also related to the ongoing calls that distinctions be made and respected between Western and Pacific epistemologies in research and praxis."[33] As they further show, there has been a change of concerns within the ecumenical approaches in the Pacific in recent decades challenged by "the globalisation of cultures and economies [that] threatens traditional social systems, structures and ethics that act as the key source for developing Pacific hermeneutical approaches to ecumenism."[34]

It is clear from the exemplary cases discussed above that the ecumenical journey in the Global South, especially in Asia and the Pacific, is strongly connected to the anti-colonial movements and the decolonising attempts of the national/regional/local churches. The Eurocentric territorial detention of the ecumenical discourse was disturbed, questioned and challenged by the local ecumenical movements in the Global South.

Theologies of *oikoumene* in the Margins

Decolonising Eurocentric Ecumenical Theologies

It is evident from the earlier discussion that the idea of ecumenism has been discerned and defined in the Global South beyond the Western framework of definitions. It is the colonial and postcolonial experiences that have been providing the foundational impetus for these *marginal* locations to move beyond the confined, rigid and fixed understanding of ecumenism of the Global North. The subterranean reality of economic exploitation and social disparity contributed significantly for the Christians in the margins to strive passionately for reimagining ecumenical theologies that not only enriched the ecumenical spirit but also challenged the ways and means the West had been imposing its *one-truth* ideologies in the name of *unity* on the non-Western Christian communities that are intrinsically diverse and multicultural. Wesley Ariarajah clearly points out that even though "Christian unity has been one of the dimensions of the understanding of the ecumenical in Asia ... the emphasis has more clearly been on the peoples, social movements, economic realities and socio-political revolutions in the Asian continent."[35] This has resulted in flooding of the distinct theologies of ecumenism in the Asian and other contexts of the Global South that displayed the churches' emphasis on justice, equality, freedom and peace. The struggles of the people in the *margins* influenced significantly on their ecumenical theology.

The twentieth century witnessed a number of prominent theological voices that made everlasting contributions not only on the notion of ecumenism but also on the ways churches around the world understood its mission and vision in the world. M.M. Thomas from India, for example, is one such theological voice that reimagined ecumenism as a prophetic movement. As the chair of the World Council of Churches Conference on Church and Society in 1966 and the moderator of the WCC's Central Committee from 1968 to 1975, Thomas did theological interventions that made a significant interrogation of the way the churches understood unity within the pretext of ecumenism. For him, the struggles for humanisation and solidarity with the people in struggle was the core for the realisation of God in *unity*. He wrote:

> [T]here can be no realisation of God and salvation of the life of the mission of the Church except in full solidarity with the world, with men in their struggles and achievements and hopes and frustrations.... [E]verything which the Church is and does should be seen within the context of what God is and does through Christ to renew the world around, and within the setting of the Church's solidarity with the world.... No style of life is Christian... 'if it is indifferent to the suffering of other people, in the victims of war and exploitation, in hungry children, in the prostitute seeking to be respected as a person, in the young man thirsting for knowledge—in all these we meet Jesus Christ.... Whether we are rich or poor, it is in solidarity with the underprivileged that our existence acquires direction and purpose.'[36]

In fact, for M.M. Thomas, ecumenism was more about solidarity in the social-margins than about unity at the church-centres. The oppressive colonial and postcolonial political contexts in which he lived instilled in him the spirit of strong nationalism and liberation. His theological emphasis on solidarity with the poor and the vulnerable influenced the ways the church understood her ecumenical solidarity, moving beyond contesting denominational differences.

As the secretary of a vibrant ecumenical body, the World Student Christian Federation, Thomas made a significant impact on the young minds of the ecumenical movements with his liberation theology. He challenged the Eurocentric notion of unity as *oneness* at the cost of prophetic divisions. Addressing an ecumenical gathering, the Student Christian Movement of India-Kerala region, in 1939, M. M. Thomas provocatively called for division in the church rather than a superficial unity. His often-cited words in that ecumenical meeting is still profound and significant:

> We youths have to create division in the Church, for redeeming the Church that it may be a fitting weapon in the hands of the Master for redeeming the world around.... What is real Church history? It is not the history of its Popes and Archbishop—no, not at all. It is the history of people who filled with the vision of a redeemed Church, created strife and division within the Church—it is the history of Luthers and Abraham Malpans— of its heretics excommunicated, of its infidels martyred, for causing revolution in the Church. If we are to be worthy of that heritage let us make quarrels and more quarrels for the sake of its redemption.[37]

These words of M.M. Thomas challenged and invited the young minds to dare to quarrel for the sake of the church. By doing so, his radical theological views upheld that unity is not about maintaining the status quo in the face of injustice, oppression and imperialism. That is why, perhaps, another Indian Christian theologian, Sathianathan Clarke, locates Thomas' theologies within a postcolonial scholarship when he says,

Perhaps Thomas can be said to be performing one important role
that is necessary in postcolonial scholarship: he lifts up the fertile,
liberation-poised, present formations of local communities,
which have future humanizing promise, instead of focusing
upon the debilitating knowledge-based, politically-funded, and
economically-driven, Western colonial strategies, which—while
being rooted in the past—have devastating present effects. There
is an unwillingness to become preoccupied with the agents that
arrive from the West through the colonial mechanism. Instead,
local agency and collective people's power become the subjects
of discernment and discourse.[38]

Augustin Ralla Ram was another prominent voice in reframing
the ecumenical theology in an Asian context. As the general
secretary of the Student Christian Association of India, Burma
and Ceylon (SCAIBC) from 1928 to 1947, and vice president
of the World Student Christian Federation (WSCF) from 1932
to 1935, Ralla Ram played a momentous role in translating
ecumenical spirit into ecumenical praxis. Writing about his
ecumenical contributions, Raj Bharat Patta, the former general
secretary of the Student Christian Movement of India, says,
"Ralla Ram throughout his life, believed, strived and participated
in promoting unity amidst affirming several diversities."[39]
Patta is right in his observation as Ralla Ram envisioned an
understanding of unity beyond the Western framework of
oneness. That is very evident in his response to Douglas Horton,
a distinguished scholar of ecumenism and professor at Harvard
Divinity School and a central committee member of the World
Council of Churches. Ralla Ram wrote,

I am afraid that my article as a reply to Dr. Horton's position
has to be very militant, for he is an outstanding leader in the
Church and the opinion which he holds is entirely contrary to
what we are attempting to do in North India by way of organic
union. As a matter of fact, Dr. Horton finds it difficult to "jump
out of his ecclesiastical skin," while we in India, who have been

given all the garden of varieties of ecclesiology, can sit down and dispassionately sort out things for ourselves.[40]

What Ralla Ram challenged in his response to Horton was the rigid ecclesial framework of organic union that was constructed within the confined and exclusivist epistemological foundations of the West. He was arguing that such constructed understanding of union does not hold any relevance to the Asian context where union is defined and practiced in the living experiences of the people. Elaborating his response, he makes a profound postcolonial critique of colonial Christianity in India that transplanted denominationalism along the lines of colonialism. He says:

> In the political world we are fighting against the unwanted imposition of the West, namely colonialism, and in the ecclesiastical world we are waging a similar battle against denominational aggrandizement. Not that the denominations have achieved no results: they have given us important emphases, but now having sufficiently emphasized various aspects of the truth, they have begun to go to seed. We are truly appalled at the rapid import of fanciful denominational inventions that emanate from the West all the time.[41]

Such a strong postcolonial interrogation coming from the Global South demanded a radical re-conceptualisation of unity, re-storying of churches' collective witness, and re-vibrating ecumenicity *contextually* and *politically*. By doing so, it strived not only to widen the ecumenical horizons, but also to deepen it in the *local* experiences of diversity and differences.

The liberation and postcolonial theologies in Asia navigated the ecumenical voyage to a different direction. Taking social justice as the prime concern of ecumenical discussions and deliberations, a number of distinct theologies from different parts of Asia provided a new dimension to the understanding of the key concepts of ecumenism such as unity, common witness, togetherness and communion. It redefined ecumenical spirituality as service to the Kingdom of God. Peter Phan sees it as the integral part of Asian ecumenism expressed by the distinct liberation theologies when he writes,

> Spirituality as service to the Kingdom of God occupies a central place in Asian theologies of liberation, such as the theologies of Choan-Seng Song, Tissa Balasuryia, Aloysius Pieris, Michael Amaladoss, Samuel Rayan, Felix Wilfred, R. S. Sugirtharajah, Carlos H. Abesamis, Aruna Gnanadason; minjung theology (Korea); homeland theology (Taiwan); the theology of struggle (the Philippines); dalit theology (India); and Asian feminist theology (Virginia Fabella, Chun Hyun Kyung, Mary John Mananzan, Kwok Pui-Lan, Elizabeth Tapia). This kind of spirituality allows Asians to overcome the pronounced individualism of their religions and ethics and to view the spiritual quest as necessarily comprising the quest for social justice.[42]

Have these concerns of the minjungs in Korea, Dalits in India, or any marginal communities in the Global South found any space in the organised ecumenical meetings, conferences, assemblies and committees? A definite 'yes' to this question is hard to give. The liberation and postcolonial theologies had to campaign in the ecumenical gatherings for their rightful place. For example, at the Vancouver assembly of the World Council of Churches in 1983, Masilamani Azariah, a Dalit theologian, had to demand a reference to the "outcastes" in the report on human rights. He argued, in fact, for the insertion of a paragraph on the plight of Dalits in India, pointing out that there were similarly marginalised groups in other places, such as the Buraku people in Japan. While migrants and refugees were included in the statement on human rights, and their rights were recognised, he demanded that Dalits certainly needed special attention. As Jesudas Athyal rightly says, "Azariah's intervention at Vancouver was, perhaps, the first time that the Dalit issue was raised at a global ecumenical platform."[43] However, Dalit theologians, like any other liberation theologians in Asia, saw the distinct Asian theologies as part of ecumenical theologies. As Deenabandhu Manchala observes,

> To some extent, one can say that ecumenical theology too, like Dalit theology, has been a counter theological discourse, an alternative to the dominant ways of theological reflection that is often grounded in western denominational/confessional ecclesial settings. Likewise, it is also faced with the need to make itself relevant to the changed realities of the twenty-first century as it is cast in and remains in the methodological mould of the twentieth century western ecclesial reality.[44]

Asian liberation theologians recognised the intriguing connection between the concerns of their theologising and of the ecumenical movement. Student movements in Asia, in particular, played a crucial role in translating such theologies in the praxis of the movement. While talking about the faith statement of Poulose Mar Poulose, a prominent ecumenical personality from Asia, George Zachariah states that "participation in the struggles of the subaltern communities such as traditional fisher people, dalits, adivasis, and women was a new baptismal experience for most of the SCMers. They discerned a new sense of 'call': a call to serve God through their involvement in social movements."[45] This was certainly the impact of the liberation theologies that made their way into the ecumenical movement. Hence, it is clear that the liberation and postcolonial theologies that emerged in different contexts of Asia contributed in understanding ecumenism as decolonisation-justice-peace-equality-oriented movement.

Women Redefining Ecumenism in Asia

"Throughout Asian ecumenical history, Christian women have
found ways to organize themselves and create structures that
give them the space to articulate their concerns and contribute
their theological and leadership skills to the church and society,"
says Aruna Gnanadason.[46] It is quite evident that women in
general and Asian women in particular have been making their
presence felt through in the history of ecumenism. To take an
example, the presence of Asian women like Sarah Chakko in
the first general assembly of the WCC in Amsterdam in 1948
made a significance impact on the way churches discerned
ecumenism. It was the Asian women's presence that contributed
to the affirmation of "the full cooperation of men and women
in the service of Christ" as integral to church unity.[47] However,
Gnanadason recognises the unfortunate fact that the history of
Christianity in general and the ecumenical historiography in Asia
in particular have been centred on the "eminent male leaders
and male theologians" sidelining the agency of women in the
ecumenical journey. While addressing the practical difficulty in
writing the history of women in the Asian ecumenical movement
and their contribution to ecumenical theological thinking, Wong
Wai Ching Angela states,

> Today, an increasing number of historians believe that the
> activities and contributions of women in most cultures and
> societies are least found in institutional records. Rather,
> alternative sources such as oral histories, private journals and
> diaries and autobiographies are given a much more important
> role in recovering the past, especially for women and the socially
> dis-privileged. Until these "unofficial" histories are explored,
> a writing of the history of women in the Asian ecumenical
> movement and their contribution to theological thinking will
> be far from complete.[48]

It is indeed true that the historiography of Christianity has been biased and unjust to women, and the ecumenical history is in no way better. This historical narratives of the ecumenical movement have failed to recognise the contributions made, the roles played and the interrogations made by women, and their histories of prophetic interventions go unrecorded. "Deeply entrenched patriarchal, ecclesial structures and power dynamics have ensured that women continue to struggle for full participation in Asian churches and ecumenical organizations."[49]

Gnanadason traces the beginning of Asian women's active involvement in the modern ecumenical movement as early as in the 1880s, especially when students and youth movements of ecumenical significance made inroads into Asia through the World Student Christian Federation (WSCF), the Young Men's Christian Association (YMCA) and the Young Women's Christian Association (YWCA). As she identifies, "from the 1970s, these associations have all included a special focus on Christian women's education and theological contributions and leadership training for active engagement in their societies. These ecumenical structures included women in leadership roles at every stage of their histories."[50]

It has to be recognised that Asian feminist/womanist theologies, which made significant contributions not only to the contextual liberation and postcolonial theologies in the Global South but also to the theologies of the churches worldwide, emerged out of their active engagements within the ecumenical movement. For example, in 1979, Marianne Katoppo,[51] a theologian from Indonesia, spoke about "Asian Theology: An Asian Woman's Perspective" at the first Asian Ecumenical Theological Conference in Sri Lanka. In the following year, in 1980, she produced her book *Compassionate and Free: An*

Asian Woman's Theology. It was one of the first books to present an Asian feminist theology using Asian myths and stories to interpret theology. She called for an ecumenical response from the Asian Christian women to the challenges that they faced both in the church and society, inviting them to seek the right to be different, be the Other, rather than having to accept identities borrowed from men and other cultures.[52]

At the same time, Asian women's radical claim for a de-imperialised theological space did not go uncriticised. When the long legacy of Western single-truth ideologies was disturbed by Asian women such as Chung Hyun Kyung of Seoul in the seventh assembly of the WCC in 1991 in Canberra, Australia, "charges of syncretism and angry debate and deep division ensued."[53] Kyung invoked the images of Shamanism and Buddhism, as well as spirits of earth, air, and water while reflecting on the Holy Spirit. While talking about Kyung's 'disturbing' and daring presentation to the ecumenical gathering in Canberra, Kwok Pui-lan, a postcolonial feminist theologian from Hong Kong, writes, "She freely employed both indigenous rituals and Asian philosophical themes and cultural motifs to articulate the hopes and aspirations of Asian people."[54] This was also a way of challenging the long-celebrated Western theologies that vehemently demonised the Asian experiences, epistemologies and spiritualities. It is evident in the context of Asia and the Pacific that Chung Hyun Kyung finds a significant place in the curriculum of theological education, thus making a lasting impact on the ecumenical discourses in the Global South.[55] Ecumenical theologies in the Global South are greatly benefited from such radical interrogations and interventions that disturbed and irked the mainstream theologies and ecumenical imaginations.

Talking about such irks and disturbances consciously caused by other Asian women in a different context, Monica Melanchthon signifies the contribution of Dalit womanist/ feminist theologies in India in reshaping the ecumenical understanding of the church. In her editorial to a special issue of *In God's Image*, an ecumenical theological journal which came out as a result of Asian women's ecumenical gatherings and deliberations, Melanchthon wrote,

> It is hoped that Dalit women's theologizing will irk, worry, disturb and bother mainstream theology. It is meant to haunt all efforts at theologizing . . . the term haunt is used in terms of a meeting place, the stomping ground of all those who suffer pain and it is at the intersection of the lives of these women characterized by pain that theology is born. Dalit womanist/ feminist theologizing is a call for self-identity and assertion. It is intensely personal in its expression.[56]

In God's Image, carrying Asian women's voices across the globe, and particularly in the ecumenical fraternity, created an ecumenical platform for women from different walks of life to share their vulnerable experiences of exploitation and dehumanisation in their own contexts. The above-mentioned issue, for example, made Dalit women's struggle for life and dignity, their stories of pain, suffering and also success, and their radical reimaginations of ecumenism known to their counterparts in other parts of Asia and elsewhere.

The immediate sociopolitical and ecclesiastical context of Asian women is of poverty, exploitation, and injustice of various forms. It is a diverse context where multiple systems work intersectionally to maintain the subjugation of caste, class, gender, sexual orientation, and so on. Asian women have been trying right from the beginning of the ecumenical movement to speak about these oppressive structures, to theologise their experiences and to challenge the church and ecumenical partners to reimagine a theology of ecumenism that makes sense to their living conditions. Hence, Asian women have constantly provided necessary tools to redefine and relive ecumenism *contextually*.

Student Ecumenical Movements in Decolonising *Oikoumene*

As it is quite evident in the history of the modern ecumenical movement, student and lay movements have played a decisive role in the early ecumenical engagements. Particularly in the Global South young people did not take ecumenism as a fashionable career or an exotic touring opportunity to explore different parts of the world. Rather, they took it as a revolutionary vocation to redeem the church from its institutional closets. As George Zachariah observes, for young people who were committed to redefine the church by breaking the denominational and territorial walls of the church, ecumenism "was an unwavering expression of collective resilience against all contemporary expressions of Empire. It was manifested in different parts of the world where Christian faith and ecumenical vision inspired young people to reject the State theology of the church (the theological justification of the status quo with its casteism, racism, capitalism and totalitarianism by misusing theological concepts and biblical texts for its own political purposes), and to join the protest movements in the public sphere against such structural sins."[57]

It is significant to note that young people saw the institutional church as prison and they believed that through the ecumenical movement they could attempt to break those prisons. The pertinent and provocative question raised in the 4th World Conference of Christian Youth, held in Lausanne in 1960, makes it evident: "Are there no revolutionaries here, people who do not want to improve or modify the structures and institutions of our Christian life, but who are ready to break out of these prisons?... who want to avoid one of the major ecumenical sins—that of being 'churchy?'"[58] The young delegates gathered at Lausanne overtly affirmed that being 'churchy' was a major 'ecumenical sin'. Chris Tremewan makes it all the more clear in his *Teatime at Revolution* by bringing in some concrete examples. He says,

> Take the experience of young Japanese Christian students in 1968 and 1969. Zenkyoto (All Campus Joint Struggle Committee) was one of the most active groups in the student revolt and had particular support among the students of Christian universities. Their understanding of their action was formed around several main concepts. Jiko hitei, which literally means self-negation, inspired the denial of students' elitist cultural formation and the normal self-image of a student as a future member of Japan's ruling class. This denial was so radical as to carry through to include the individual's assent to "the system". Genten e no tachi kaeri, or "return to the original point", referred mainly to the raison d'etre of the university which had been perverted by the role given it in a society dominated by monopoly capitalism.[59]

At a time when the denominational and ecumenical church youth work was seen as "a recruitment technique to draft young people into the activities and consciousness of conventional religion," Tremewan says that it had "come under increasing criticism from youth active in movements for social justice. They see it as functioning to co-opt and undermine surges of the human spirit amongst young people because it destines them to become juvenile imitations of their religious mentors... In many Asian and South Pacific situations, Christian youth work has become the focus of such a critique."[60] Such examples clearly show how the imperial nature of ecumenical movement was at work. By trying to co-opt young people to its service the ecumenical movement not only betrayed its ecumenical vision, but also corrupted its faith. Zachariah rightly traces such imperial nature of the ecumenical movement even in our times. As he says,

> Ecumenism has become a lucrative career for many, and ecumenical leadership has the potential to become imperial and exclusive. Ecumenical documents and statements have become archival materials for research and publications without any influence on the mission and witness of the member churches. With the cooption of the ecumenical movements by the churches and the powerful lobbies, ecumenical involvement has become a stepping stone for ecumenical empire building. Today we lost the politics of the reign of God. We are all infected by the politics of ecumenical career building.[61]

However, young people in the history of the ecumenical movement have been so committed to redeem the church and the ecumenical movement from its sin of being imperial. For that, the Asia Youth Assembly, jointly organised by the World Student Christian Federation's (WSCF) Asia Pacific Region and the Christian Conference of Asia Youth in Delhi in 1984, stands as a good example. As Tremewan describes, "The great promise of the Asian ecumenical youth movement is that it might get completely out of control. *Out of control* of church leaders and the ecumenical mafia, *out of control* of funding agencies and project networks, *out of control* of compromised church-state relationships and corrupt elitist theology."[62] The call to get out of control was also resonated in the opening address of the chairperson of the WSCF Asia Pacific Region, Bishop Poulose Mar Poulose:

> In this situation what shall be the role of Christian youth? I would say that they should be a dissenting minority; they should be non-conformists. If we learn lessons from the life style of Jesus and the community life of early Christians, we will be compelled to stand as the community of Jesus, as a dynamic force within the society, acting as a dissenting minority. To live as a

dissenting minority is never the same as the present tendency to foster minority consciousness among Asian Christians. Rather it means to involve ourselves with the aspirations of the people of the land for a better future, to raise a dissenting voice against the oppressive forces of our time.[63]

These historical examples make it evident that the student/youth movements within the ecumenical journey had always been nonconformist and revolutionary in decolonising the imperial ecumenical movement. The question, if the contemporary ecumenical youth student movements carry this revolutionary heritage of nonconformist tradition and challenge the empires of our time, is a difficult one to answer. The contemporary youth student movements within the ecumenical movement seem to have lost that tradition. Either they are aligning with the 'evangelical' movements, placing exclusive emphasis on individual salvation and personal piety, or they are co-opting the mainstream dominant ecumenical movement. A close look at the few recent theological and ecumenical statements that came out of the different ecumenical youth gatherings make it quite evident. To name an example:

"A message from the Echos Commission on Youth in the Ecumenical Movement" in 2008 reads as follows:

As young people, we join with Christian sisters and brothers of all ages who work and pray for the healing of the nations (c.f. Revelation 22:2). We pray especially that God would raise up young people who empower themselves and are empowered by others as agents of this transformation. With renewed faith, passion, and commitment, let us continue the intergenerational and collaborative work to which we have been called in the churches and throughout the ecumenical movement.[64]

A pious approach to the contextual issues and problems echoed in the above statement does not seem to reflect the radical and revolutionary spirit that the earlier ecumenical youth movements had. Moreover, youths asserting to work in 'collaboration' with the mainstream ecumenism and denominations pose the danger of co-option. Students/youths need to raise uncomfortable questions to the dominant ecumenical movement and to experiment alternative models of being ecumenical in the world.

Ecumenism and the Expression of Diversity

One of the unique and distinct features of Asia is the reality of multireligious and multifaith coexistence. This has its own place in the ecumenical movement of the churches of different geographical origins. Hendrik Kraemer, in his presentation, *The Christian Message in a Non Christian World*, to the ecumenical gathering in Tambaram, warned the churches of Asia and Africa about the dangers of syncretism, and denying revelatory truth and experience of God in non-Christian religions.[65] While challenging such an approach, David G. Moses, who was the president of the National Christian Council of India, called it a false approach. As M.M. Thomas pointed out,

> …He (David Moses) disagrees with Kraemer's sole pre-occupation with revelation as occurrence which reduces other religions to "human efforts to understand the totality of existence." Moses saw valid revelation and the religious experience of God in other religions which make dialogue about contents and apologetics meaningful, and maintained the uniqueness of the Christian revelation as defendable rationally and philosophically….[66]

This shows clearly that the ecumenical gatherings provided a potential platform for the early debates on the possibility and inevitability of ecumenical engagements with the inter-religious dialogue.

Stanely J. Samartha was an important ecumenical voice from Asia who "prepared, shaped, and implemented a new approach of the ecumenical movement to peoples of other religious traditions."[67] It is noteworthy that after the Uppsala assembly, the World Council of Churches Commission on World Mission and Evangelism asked Samartha to pursue a study on "The Word of God and the Living Faiths of Men."[68] Being the founding director of WCC's sub-unit on dialogue with people of living faiths, "Samartha's personal traits and qualities contributed a great deal in removing some of the initial hesitations many Hindus had about Christians wanting suddenly to engage in dialogue with them. He did much to remove the prejudice among many Hindus and Buddhists that dialogue is yet another tool in Christian zeal for evangelism."[69] This was taken further by another significant ecumenical personality from Sri Lanka, Wesley Ariarajah, who served the ecumenical movement as the director of the WCC's inter-religious dialogue programme for many years. He urged the ecumenical fraternity around the world to take interfaith dialogue as the key commitment of ecumenism and he continues to be a strong proponent of interfaith dialogue.[70]

As Jesudas Athyal rightly points out,

> [T]he presence of ecumenical study centres that focused on inter-faith relations was a significant development in South Asia during the post-colonial period. The Christian Institute for the Study of Religion and Society in Bangalore (India), the Henry Martyn Institute of Islamic Studies in Hyderabad (India), the Ecumenical Institute for Study and Dialogue in Colombo (Sri Lanka), and the Christian Institute of Sikh Studies in Batala, Punjab (India) all played a key role in shaping the ecumenical discourse in the churches of the region about inter-faith relations.[71]

He also identifies that in the rapidly changing religio-political context of Pakistan, "the Christian Study Centre in Rawalpindi seeks to help churches obtain a better understanding of their

historical background and existence as a part of the universal
church and their particular calling in an Islamic state in the
midst of a process of Islamization in the country."[72]

The Asian contribution towards the interfaith engagements
within the ecumenical movement should be seen not only as
a new dimension of ecumenism, but also an Asian challenge
towards the Eurocentric logic of oneness that shaped and
dominated the theology of oikumene. Moving beyond the
rigid borders of single-strandic theology of the Christendom
and embracing and celebrating the multiplicity and manyness
manifested in the 'other' was indeed radical and anti-imperial.
Even today the multifaith realities of Asia and other parts of the
Global South constantly remind our ecumenical engagements
to be rooted in the fluid logic of manyness and multiplicity by
being essentially multi-strandic.

Conclusion

Ecumenism in Asia and the Pacific has indeed been a decolonising
movement challenging the territorial nature of the ecumenical
movement. The marginal epistemologies and practices of
ecumenism subverted the colonial face of ecumenism. Bringing
in evidences from Asian and Oceanic Christianity, this chapter
concludes that a deterritorialisation of ecumenism happened
by challenging Western dominance in the ecumenical journey
of the churches. It is clear from the above discussions that for
Asia and the Pacific, ecumenism is still a vibrant and living
phenomenon. Yet, there is a need to reimagine the ecumenical
journey in order to make it more vibrant and relevant.

Endnotes

[1] For example, Ahn Kyo-Seong, though tries to revisit the ecumenical
movement from the perspective of the Korean Church, believes that "...the

ecumenical movement was born and grown in the context of the modern missionary movement of the Western Church." See, Ahn Kyo-Seong, "The Asian Context and the Ecumenical Movement of the Korean Church," *Korean Presbyterian Journal of Theology* Vol. 45, No. 3 (2013): 37-61; here 41; Mathew George Chunakara, the present General Secretary of the Christian Conference of Asia, nullifying the church-historian T.V. Philip's assertion that "the real impetus for ecumenism came from Asia," argues that "the concrete steps of the 20th-century ecumenical developments in Asia were mainly due to the influences from the West after the formation of the IMC in 1910 and the work of its continuation committee under the leadership of John R. Mott." See, Mathew George Chunakara, "The Ecumenical Movement in Asia and Emerging Challenges. The Christian Conference of Asia at 60 and Beyond," *The Ecumenical Review* 69/4 (December 2017): 448-461; here 451.

[2] T. V. Philip. 1994. *Ecumenism in Asia.* Delhi: ISPCK & CSS. 144.

[3] The term Global South, in this book, is preferred as a metaphor to denote the marginal locations in the history of ecumenical movement. The ecumenical history is evident that Asia, Pacific, Africa and Latin America are considered as the 'other' of the Eurocentric ecumenical axis of power. Some of the regions specified in this regional classification may be imperial in nature and thus oppressive, but in the ecumenical power equation, they are always pushed to the margins.

[4] Kim Caroline Sanecki, "Protestant Christian Missions, Race and Empire: The World Missionary Conference of 1910, Edinburgh, Scotland," Unpublished Doctoral Dissertation submitted to the Department of History of the Georgia State University, 2016. Retrieved from: https://scholarworks.gsu.edu/history_theses/10.

[5] World Missionary Conference, 1910. Report of Commission I: *Carrying the Gospel to all the Non=Christian World.* Edinburgh and London: Oliphant, Anderson & Ferrier; New York, Chicago and Toronto: Fleming H. Revell Company, 1910: 32. [Hereinafter WMC Commission]

[6] WMC Commission I: 33.

[7] John R. Mott, *The Evangelization of the World in This Generation.* New York: Student Volunteer Movement for Foreign Missions, 1900: 32.

[8] WMC Commission I: 35.

[9] For instance, John R. Mott, though he was critical about "nominally Christian powers" for their mistreatment of non-Christians, citing the forced opium trade in China as an example, saw it as an obstacle to evangelise

the lands that are hurt by the ill effects of imperialism. John R. Mott, *The Evangelization of the World in This Generation*. New York: Student Volunteer Movement for Foreign Missions, 1900: 31-32.

[10] Theresa Carino, "Chinese Churches and the Ecumenical Movement from an Asian Perspective," *The Ecumenical Review* 69/4 (December 2017): 542-556; here 545.

[11] *The History and Records of the Conference Together with Addresses Delivered at the Evening Meetings. World Missionary Conference 1910* (Edinburgh: Oliphant, Anderson & Ferrier, n.d), 306.

[12] Tosh Arai and T. K. Thomas, "Christian Conference of Asia," in *Dictionary of the Ecumenical Movement,* edited by Nicholas Lossky et al. Second Edition. Geneva: WCC Publications, 2002, 169-170.

[13] Wati Longchar, "Ecumenical Movement in Asia: Can we Make a Difference?" *CTC Bulletin* 23/3 (August 2007): 109-114. Retrieved from: https://www.cca.org.hk/ctc/ctc07-02/12_wati_longchar109.pdf

[14] M. M. Thomas, "An Assessment of Tambaram's Contribution to the Search of the Asian Churches for an Authentic Selfhood," *International Review of Mission* 77/307 (July 1988): 390-397; here 393.

[15] George Oommen, "Challenging Identity and Crossing Borders: Unity in the Church of South India," *Word & World* 25/1 (2015), 60.

[16] Even though the nomenclature *the Communion of Churches in India* has been in use since 2004, the effort for such a communion dates back to 1952 when the episcopal synod of the Mar Thoma Church, under the leadership of Metropolitan Juhanon Mar Thoma, issued a statement calling the churches in India to unite. See Juhanon Mar Thoma, *Christianity in India and a Brief History of the Mar Thoma Church*. Tiruvalla: CSS, 2011, 73–74. Also see Jesudas M. Athyal, "The South Asian Presence in the Ecumenical Movement," *The Ecumenical Review* 69/4 (December 2017): 557-569.

[17] Jesudas M. Athyal, "The South Asian Presence in the Ecumenical Movement," 559-560.

[18] New Delhi Statement on Unity, and Orthodox Response, Third Assembly of the WCC, New Delhi, 1961. Retrieved from: www.wcc-coe.org/wcc/who/crete-o2-e.html

[19] Norman Goodall, ed., *The Uppsala Report 1968: Official Report of the Fourth Assembly of the World Council of Churches, Uppsala, July 4-20, 1968* (Geneva: World Council of Churches, 1968), 365-366.

[20] See the Report of the Reference Committee, in Michael Kinnamon, ed., *Sings of the Spirit: Official Report Seventh Assembly, Canberra, Australia, 7-20 February 1991* (Geneva: World Council of Churches, 1991), 175-176.

[21] An interesting study by Manoj Kumar Mishra shows how in the modern states elite sections of a community cleverly use nationalism discourse to foster their own elite interest by camouflaging it under the Enlightenment ideas of equality, liberty and justice and welfare of the subaltern masses. See, Manoj Kumar Mishra, "Elite, Nationalism and Nation-States," *International Studies of Humanities and Social Science Studies*, Vol. 3, Issue 1, July 2016: 95-103.

[22] Wati Longchar, "Ecumenical Movement in Asia: Can we Make a Difference?", 112.

[23] Ahn Kyo-Seong, "The Asian Context and the Ecumenical Movement of the Korean Church," 43-45.

[24] Pacific Church Leaders Meeting. "Sowing a New Seed of Pacific Ecumenism". Unpublished Statement of Basis and Resolution issued in Nadi, 12 October 2017.

[25] Tevita Havea, "Uncharted Course in Familiar Waters." Unpublished paper presented at the Pacific Conference of Churches 11th General Assembly, Auckland, New Zealand: October 2018.

[26] Fele Nokise, "Ecumenism and its Hermeneutical Experience in Oceania," *The Pacific Journal of Theology* Series II No. 46, 2011: 95-127; here 95.

[27] It is important to note that the year 1961 is significant also for other reasons, especially in the ecumenical movement. The third Assembly of the World Council of Churches took place in the same year in New Delhi in India, another location in the Global South providing a newer impetus of a paradigm shift in ecumenical thinking.

[28] Fele Nokise, "Ecumenism and its Hermeneutical Experience in Oceania," 97.

[29] See Pacific Conference of Churches, "Rethinking the Household of God in the Pacific: Concept Paper for Church Leaders," 2010, http://www.actnowpng.org/sites/default/files/Re-thinking%20Oceania%20pc.pdf

[30] Anna Anisi and Aisake Casimira, "An Historical Overview of Ecumenical Formation and Development" in *Navigating Troubled Waters: The Ecumenical Movement in the Pacific Islands Since the 1980s,* edited by Manfred Ernst and Lydia Johnson, (Suva, Fiji: PTC, 2017), 15.

[31] For a detailed study on this, see Charles W. Forman, T*he Voice of Many Waters: The Story of the Life and Ministry of the Pacific Conference of Churches in the Last 25 Years* (Suva: Lotu Pasifika Productions, 1986).

[32] Faitala Talapusi, "The Future of Theology in the Pacific," Paper Presented at the EATWOT Conference, Suva, Fiji, September 14, 1994, 1.

[33] Anna Anisi and Aisake Casimira, "An Historical Overview of Ecumenical Formation and Development," 28. The authors draw our attention to some examples as foundation for their analysis: Alexander Mamak and Grant McCall, eds., *Paradise Postponed: Essays on Research and Development in the South Pacific* (Rushcutters Bay, AU: Pergamon Press, 1978); Epeli Hau ofa, "Our Sea of Islands," in *A New Oceania: Rediscovering our Sea of Islands*, edited by Eric Waddell, Vijay Naidu, and Epeli Hau ofa, (Suva: University of the South Pacific, 1993); and Larry Thomas, "Vaka Vuku: Navigating Knowledge," paper presented, Pacific Epistemologies Conference, University of the South Pacific, Suva, Fiji, July 3-7, 2006.

[34] Anna Anisi and Aisake Casimira, "An Historical Overview of Ecumenical Formation and Development," 28.

[35] Wesley Ariarajah, "Ecumenism in Asia as Interfaith Dialogue–A Historical Survey," in Asian Handbook for Theological Education and Ecumenism, edited by Hope Antone et al. (Oxford: Regnum Books, 2013), 228.

[36] M.M. Thomas, "The Cross and the Kingdom of God," in *New Creation in Christ* (Delhi: ISPCK, 1976), 63-65.

[37] M. M. Thomas, *Ideological Quest within Christian Commitment*, Bangalore/Madras: CISRS/CLS, 1983, 29-30.

[38] Sathianathan Clarke, "M. M. Thomas," in *Empire and the Christian Tradition: New Readings of Classical Theologians*, edited by Kwok Pui-lan, Don H. Compier, and Joerg Rieger (Minneapolis, Minn.: Fortress Press, 2007), 434.

[39] Raj Bharath Patta, "'Lengthen Thy Cords and Strengthen Thy Stakes': Augustine Ralla Ram's Ecumenical Missional Contributions," in *A Light to the Nations. The Indian Presence in the Ecumenical Movement in the Twentieth Century*, edited by Jesudas M. Athyal (Geneva: World Council of Churches, 2016), 53.

[40] Augustine Ralla Ram, "Organic Church Unity: A Comment from India," *The Ecumenical Review*, 8/3 (April 1956): 243-248; here 243.

[41] Augustine Ralla Ram, "Organic Church Unity: A Comment From India," 244.

[42] Peter C. Phan, "Christian Social Spirituality: A Global Perspective," in *Catholic Social Justice: Theological and Practical Explorations*, edited by Philomena Cullen, Bernard Hoose, and Gerard Mannion (New York: Continuum, 2007), 33.

[43] Jesudas M. Athyal, "The South Asian Presence in the Ecumenical Movement," 565.

[44] Deenabandhu Manchala, "Expanding the Ambit: Dalit Theological Contribution to Ecumenical Social Thought," in *Dalit Theology in the Twenty-first Century: Discordant Voices, Discerning Pathways,* edited by Sathianathan Clarke, Deenabandhu Manchala, and Philip Vinod Peacock (New Delhi: Oxford University Press, 2011), 41.

[45] George Zachariah, "Poulose Mar Poulose: An Activist of Alternative Ecumenism" in *A Light to the Nations. The Indian Presence in the Ecumenical Movement in the Twentieth Century*, edited by Jesudas M. Athyal (Geneva: World Council of Churches, 2016), 157.

[46] Aruna Gnanadason, "Asian Women in the Ecumenical Movement Voices of Resistance and Hope," *The Ecumenical Review* 16/4 (December 2017): 516-526; here 516.

[47] *Man's Disorder and God's Design,* 5 vols., vol. 5: *The First Assembly of the World Council of Churches, held at Amsterdam, August 22ⁿᵈ to September 4ᵗʰ, 1948*, edited by W. A. Visser't Hooft. The Amsterdam Assembly Series (New York: Harper & Brothers, 1948), 146.

[48] Wong Wai Ching Angela, "Women Doing Theology with the Asian Ecumenical Movement," in *A History of the Ecumenical Movement in Asia*, Vol. 2, edited by Ninan Koshy (Hong Kong: WSCF AP, YMCA & CCA, 2004), 86.

[49] Aruna Gnanadason, "Asian Women in the Ecumenical Movement Voices of Resistance and Hope," 517.

[50] Aruna Gnanadason, "Asian Women in the Ecumenical Movement Voices of Resistance and Hope," 517.

[51] Marianne Katoppo served the ecumenical idea as a member of the Ecumenical Association of Third World Theologians (EATWOT), and was part of the executive committee of the Indonesian National Council of Churches.

[52] See Marianne Katoppo, *Compassionate and Free: An Asian Woman's Theology*, Maryknoll, New York: Orbis, 1980.

[53] Melanie Duguid-May, "The Ecumenical Movement," in *History of Global Christianity*, Volume III, *History of Christianity in the 20ᵗʰ Century*, edited by Jens Holger Schjorring, Norman A. Hjelm and Kevin Ward, Leiden, Boston: Brill, 2016: 147-181; here 179.

[54] Kwok Pui-lan, *Introducing Asian Feminist Theology* (Sheffield: Sheffield Academic Press, 2000), 25.

[55] Both in the Pacific and in India, in the ecumenical theological institutions, Chung Hyun Kyung's book, which she published one year prior to the Canberra Assembly, is well read and has been playing a significant role in shaping the understanding of contextual theologies. Chung Hyun Kyung, *Struggle to be the Sun Again. Introducing Asian Women's Theology*, Maryknoll, NY: Orbis, 1990.

[56] Monica Melanchthon, "The Editorial: The Haunts of Pain: Theologizing Dalits," *In God's Image* 26:3 (September 2007): 1-8; here 1.

[57] George Zachariah, "Poulose Mar Poulose: An Activist of Alternative Ecumenism", 159.

[58] http://www.oikoumene.org/en/programmes/the-wcc-and-the-ecumenical-movement-in-the-21st-century/youth-in-the-ecumenical-movement/history-of-youth-and-the-wcc.html. As cited by George Zachariah, "Poulose Mar Poulose: An Activist of Alternative Ecumenism," 160.

[59] Chris Tremewan, *Teatime at the Revolution*, Hong Kong: WSCF Asia Pacific, 1983, 130.

[60] Chris Tremewan, *Teatime at the Revolution*, 12.

[61] George Zachariah, "Poulose Mar Poulose: An Activist of Alternative Ecumenism," 160.

[62] Chris Tremewen, Out of Control: The Official Report of the Asia Youth Assembly, Hong Kong: CCA Youth, 1985. As cited by George Zachariah, "Poulose Mar Poulose: An Activist of Alternative Ecumenism," 161.

[63] Paulose Mar Paulose, "Be a Dissenting Minority," in Tremewen, Out of Control, Op cit. As cited by George Zachariah, "Poulose Mar Poulose: An Activist of Alternative Ecumenism," 161.

[64] https://www.oikoumene.org/en/resources/documents/commissions/youth/voices-of-youth-stronger-and-better-heard. Accessed on 15 July 2020.

⁶⁵ M. M. Thomas and P. T. Thomas, *Towards an Indian Christian Theology* (Tiruvalla, India: CLS, 1992), 192.

⁶⁶ M. M. Thomas and P. T. Thomas, *Towards an Indian Christian Theology* (Tiruvalla, India: CLS, 1992), 193.

⁶⁷ Jesudas M. Athyal, "The South Asian Presence in the Ecumenical Movement," 561.

⁶⁸ Melanie Duguid-May, "The Ecumenical Movement," 167.

⁶⁹ Wesley Ariarajah, "The Pioneering Ministry of Stanley J. Samartha," in *A Light to the Nations: The Indian Presence in the Ecumenical Movement in the Twentieth Century,* edited by Jesudas M. Athyal (Geneva: WCC Publications, 2016), 129.

⁷⁰ See, Wesley Ariarajah, *Strangers or Co-Pilgrims: The Impact of Interfaith Dialogue on Christian Faith and Practice* (Minneapolis: Fortress Press, 2017).

⁷¹ Jesudas M. Athyal, "The South Asian Presence in the Ecumenical Movement," 561.

⁷² Jesudas M. Athyal, "The South Asian Presence in the Ecumenical Movement," 561.

CHAPTER 4

Reimagining *Oikoumene*

Introduction

Chapter One of this book problematised the concept and definitions of *oikoumene* and demanded a reimagination and redefinition to make it relevant for the diverse contexts of Asia and the Pacific. This chapter provides some possible reimaginations drawing lessons from the previous discussions and also from the wider context and history of ecumenism. Looking at the biblical roots of the idea of *oikoumene*, this chapter attempts to redeem the colonial implications embedded in ecumenical discourses. Drawing some lessons from the history of Christianity, various possible alternatives are proposed.

Resisting and Reclaiming Biblical Notion of *Oikoumene*

The term *oikoumene* appears in various books of the New Testament, especially Revelation, Acts and the Gospels. The New Testament does not propose a singular meaning of this term in its appearances in different texts. Whereas in Revelation the term appears three times, in Luke and Acts it appears eight times. According to scholars, the meaning of the usage of the term varies from text to text. David Aune believes that the references to *oikoumene* in Revelation are synonymous with "the inhabitants of the earth," *oikoumene* having primarily a geographical meaning.[1] However, the Gospels and Acts associate *oikoumene* with the Roman Empire and hence, they pose a challenge to radically redefine the notion of *oikoumene* from the point of view of the colonised. To state a few examples: Luke situates Jesus' birth alongside August's imperial declaration in Luke 2:1: "In those days a decree went out from Caesar Augustus that the whole *oikoumene* should be enrolled." In the so-called temptation narrative, Luke uses the word *oikoumene* again when Satan 'offers' to give Jesus the kingdoms of the *oikoumene* (4:5). Matthew also uses the term in 24:13-14: "And the gospel of the kingdom will be preached in the whole *oikoumene,* as a testimony to all nations." And in the same context Luke also uses the term when he writes: "There will be distress of nations… people fainting with fear and with foreboding of what is coming upon the *oikoumene*" (Luke 21:25-26).

All these usages of the term *oikoumene* strictly refer to the Roman Empire and hence do not subscribe to the modern usage of *oikoumene* as God's creation of a household for all inhabited world. However, it is important to read the biblical texts that refer to the *oikoumene* of Rome in a political sense implying that the New Testament writers envisaged and foretold the end of Roman Empire. The faith in the end of a political empire is also a faith in the beginning of a redeemed *oikoumene* that breaks the imperial borders and becomes an inclusive and democratic household of all. However, as Rossing cautions, any attempt "to reclaim or redefine the word oikoumene for the agenda of ecumenism must begin by repudiating the imperial trajectory of the word, including the church's own imperial legacy."[2] Therefore, when the modern ecumenical discourses are located within such a complex notion of *oikoumene* we need to strive for reimagining *oikoumene* without perpetuating an imperial view.

Shift in the Theology of *Oikoumene*

As discussed in the previous chapter, the early modern ecumenical gatherings, especially in the first half of the twentieth century, deliberated theologically on being Christ-centred and church-centred. Ecumenical theologies vehemently attempted to universalise Christ and proclaimed that the universal nature of Christ would appropriate him to all other cultures of the world. Hence the universality of Christ and the Christian gospel were passionately affirmed. The unity among Christian denominations were sought, mainly to achieve carrying the gospel "to evangelize the world in this generation."[3]

However, a new outlook to the theology of *oikoumene* took shape mainly in the latter part of the twentieth century thanks to the World War political scenario that paved the way for freedom movements across the world. It had an impact on global Christianity in general and Christianity in the non-Western world particularly. Especially, the non-Western Christian communities started to be self-critical about their dependence on the Western imperial forces, including Christian missions, and started to be part of the freedom movements and the movements of rebuilding independent nations like India.[4] The formation of the World Council of Churches and other international and regional ecumenical establishments initiated the discussion on the Christian role in the formation of a responsible society.[5] The Second Vatican Council, or Vatican II, also had played an important role in the shift in the understanding of ecumenism.[6]

Another major shift in the theology of *oikoumene* has to be credited to the emergence of liberation theology and its focus on the preferential option for the poor. These political and social discourses shifted the emphasis of ecumenism from "Christian unity for evangelising the world in this generation" to the participation in the struggles of the marginalised and oppressed people in different parts of the world. It was also the time that the new world economic order emerged based on the internationalisation of capital and labour. Western countries began to exercise their economic domination on the 'Third World countries'. In such a crucial shift in the global political scenario, the ecumenical movement redefined its faith and theology in solidarity with the struggles of the marginalised and started to theologise the struggles of the Asian, African, Latin American and Pacific people.

As Agnes Abuom, the Moderator of the Central Committee of the World Council of Churches, remembers the focus of the WCC Assembly held in Uppsala in 1968 in her address to the Swedish Ecumenical Weekend in 2018:

> That pivotal year in politics, popular culture, and geopolitics also ushered in a new era for the worldwide ecumenical movement and the World Council of Churches. Its 4th Assembly, held in June in Uppsala, Sweden, decisively shifted the WCC into social engagements on the world's stage.[7]

In this phase, the ecumenical movement started theologically engaging its commitment to social causes in order to fight against racism, poverty and economic injustice. Eventually the theology of ecumenism started to engage in the larger questions of the non-Western societies such as decolonisation, anti-war movements and ecological concerns. Those concerns started to challenge the Eurocentric theology of the ecumenical movements to shift its foci from church-centredness to people-centred theological engagements.[8] Konrad Raiser calls it a shift from an anthropocentric vision to a life-centred vision.[9] This way the ecumenical movement redefined the meaning of *oikoumene* in the wider sense of solidarity and unity, which is also popularly called *wider ecumenism*. Since then ecumenism has been defined in the wider sense of relationships that encompasses the integrity of whole creation. In a way, it was an initiative to redefine the meaning of *oikoumene* relevantly by rejecting the foundationalist epistemology of the modern ecumenical missiology and theology.[10] It was an effort to go beyond the humanistic, existentialist, essentialist and liberationist foundations of modern epistemology and acknowledge the political and epistemological difference of the various life worlds. Of course, *oikoumene* in the latter part of the world church history has become a counter-imagination of unity in the context of fragmentation, marginalisation and globalisation.

Oikoumene of Oneness to *Oikoumene* of Manyness

Some of the most vocal critiques of the use of the term *oikoumene* within the ecumenical movement today are being raised by critics of economic globalisation. The Harare assembly of the World Council of Churches includes in its message an appendix of globalisation contrasting the global market's "*oikoumene* of domination" with the "*oikoumene* of faith and solidarity that motivates and energizes the ecumenical movement."[11] Likewise, the Lutheran World Federation document on the global economy condemns globalisation's hegemonic view of *oikoumene* and proposes instead an alternative vision of *oikoumene* that values plurality and cultural diversity:

> Globalization brings a competing vision of the *Oikoumene*, the unity of humankind. But the unity of humankind being promoted

by globalization is one of exploitation and domination, while the unity envisaged by the *Oikoumene* is one characterized by solidarity and justice. Our vision of the *Oikoumene* puts great value in plurality and cultural diversity for mutual enrichment and for affirmation of life experiences as expressed in different traditions.[12]

Even though such reimaginations of *oikoumene* bring radical dimensions to our contemporary ecumenical understandings, the idea of plurality and diversity cannot be taken independently without its association with the Western imperial notion of *unity*. There is still the problem of the Christian kyriarchal use of the term through history. One should not forget that "Christian ecumenical councils historically have embraced hierarchical and centralized models of unity in the *oikoumene* more along the lines of…Roman rule—'organizing the whole *oikoumene* as a single household'—rather than models of unity that respect plurality and cultural diversity."[13]

It needs to be remembered that the emperor Constantine convened the first ecumenical council because he did not want to allow difference or dissent in the *oikoumene*. As discussed in the first chapter, imperial Rome imposed its vision of a united *oikoumene* by means of military conquest. Thus, in order to reimagine *oikoumene* today we must reject any kyriarchal models of unity. The ecumenical history of the Roman Empire and of modern Western Christianity reminds us that those at the centre will tend to construct a single unified household in which those at the margins are silenced for the sake of unity and universality. By contrast, we must seek decentralised models that stand with those at the margins of the *oikoumene*, advocating what Brazilian theologian Vitor Westhelle calls a "strong case for a weak ecclesiology."[14]

Ecumenical documents often see diversity and disunity as a 'problem' in order to urge more 'visible unity.' For example, WCC declared in its 7th Assembly in 1991 that,

> Diversities which are rooted in theological traditions, various cultural, ethnic or historical contexts are integral to the nature of communion; yet there are limits to diversity. Diversity is illegitimate when, for instance, it makes impossible the common confession of Jesus Christ as God and Savior the same yesterday, today, and tomorrow....[15]

Further, the same Assembly comes out with a definition of unity:

> The unity of the Church to which we are called is a koinonia given and expressed in the common confession of the apostolic faith; a common sacramental life entered by the one baptism and celebrated together in one eucharistic fellowship; a common life in which members and ministries are mutually recognised and reconciled; and a common mission witnessing to the gospel of God's grace to all people and serving the whole of creation. The goal of the search for full communion is realised when all the churches are able to recognise in one another the one, holy, catholic and apostolic church in its fullness.[16]

Such discourses need a critical intervention. Who decides which diversity is illegitimate and which one legitimate? What is *common confession, common life, common mission*? Does it not resemble the Roman *oikoumene* discourse imposing one *common* absolute way of living and expressing one's faith/tradition/culture? It is in this context that ecumenist Konrad Raiser questions whether unity in the *oikoumene* today can even be considered a desirable goal:

> "Unity"...still seems to have an unquestioned positive ring in the ecumenical movement....The notion of unity is part of a pattern of mind which has entered Christian thinking and practice through its inculturation in the classical Greco-Roman world.... The orientation of thinking and practice towards achieving and

maintaining unity almost inevitably leads to hierarchichal systems of order which feminist analysis has described as one of the crucial features of "patriarchy...." In view of this questionable ancestry of the key notion of "unity," it is surprising that the question has been so seldom asked as to whether it is a suitable concept to express the ecumenical vision.[17]

Raiser recommends rather the goal of *koinonia* that recognises and values sharing and partnership in the *ekklesia*. As he notes, the image of *koinonia* is widely embraced within the ecumenical movement today that can address economic disparities in the *oikoumene* as well as deepen communion across theological and ethnic diversities.[18] Marlene Perera, a Roman Catholic theologian from Sri Lanka, describes the *ekklesia* in the Asian setting as multiplicity—women, men, children interacting together—rooted in local community:

> I see not one church but a multiplicity of churches that have been baptized by and taken root in the different faces of numerous human communities, manifesting the richness of the face of the immanent God walking with us on this pilgrimage. In this perspective it is the local church in all its richness and weakness which enters into deep communion with other churches, thus manifesting another profound visage of God. Communion is their unity in diversity.[19]

Identifying the logic of oneness as an important crisis that the ecumenical movement is facing today, Y.T. Vinayaraj, a Dalit Theologian, proposes the logic of manyness as an alternative imagination. He argues that "the logic of manyness dismantles the logic of oneness."[20] Realising the possibility of the logic of manyness meaning an anarchical pluralism that makes being together impossible, he affirms that it does not promote an anarchical pluralism, because it is an experience of 'multiplicity' which cannot be reduced to One. This has been the major focus of the forgoing pages. The celebration of manyness and multiplicity, particularly in the colonial and postcolonial contexts of the Global South, is evidently visible in their ecumenical journey. What is distinct in this journey is the place of the margins. The logic of manyness is strongly rooted in the margins which were once the ecumenical and missional 'other' of the Western Christianity. The new stories of ecumenism that resonate from the marginal experiences redefine the margins as the redemptive spaces and thus affirm the potential agency of the margins in redeeming the *oikoumene* from its colonial captivity of the logic of oneness.

Oikoumene: A Movement Towards Deterritorialising Christianity

Within the ecumenical theological arena, study on Christianity was much discussed. World Christianity has been used as a trendy term in the last few decades within ecumenical discourses. As a movement of Christianity, it has experienced many transitions in its path. I would focus on three important transitions or shifts in this movement and problematise them for a better understanding of world Christianity in our plury-expressional ecumenical context today.

1.   Ecumenism of the Contemporary Christianity

Leslie Newbegin, for example, used the term *contemporary Christianity* to denote Christianity beyond the Western normative category. Sathianathan Clarke identifies the term "contemporary Christianity" as one of the momentous shifts in looking at global Christianity.[21] Newbegin, after the 1980s, attempted to communicate the implications of Christian witness in religiously plural India to the secularising West, especially in ecumenical gatherings. "Contemporary Christianity," in this sense, meant to understand regional Christianities and their potentiality in being transformed into global Christianity.[22] Clarke rightly highlights that the drawback of this term is that "it is vulnerable to being equated with what is currently popular in the Western world."[23] The usage of the term "contemporary Christianity" often tends to view regional Christianities in Africa, Asia, the Pacific, and Latin America through the lenses of Western Christianity. Western Christian territory, in this usage, becomes the standard in understanding and analysing the current Christian expressions in the non-Western territories of the world.

2.   *Ecumenism in the non-Western World/Post-Western Christianity*

Another major shift in the study of Christianity as an ecumenical effort could be traced to the usage of the phrase "Christianity in the non-Western World" or "post-Western Christianity." For example, the University of Edinburgh Divinity School named its new centre in 1982 as the Centre for the Study of Christianity in the Non-Western World, which was renamed later as the Centre for the Study of World Christianity. The purpose of this centre is stated as "to advance high-quality scholarship in Christianity as a polycentric faith whose adherents are now far more numerous in the majority world than in Europe or North America."[24] Since 1995 the university also has published a pioneering journal that includes this name in its title, *Studies in World Christianity*. "Christianity in the non-Western World" focused on expanding the corpus of Christianity by 'studying' neglected or unfocused expressions of Christianity in the world.[25] Quite a noteworthy shift, indeed! However, this terminology tends to territorialise the object of study as non-Western or post-Western, the 'other' of the Western-self. Under this term the West started to analyse the non-West with the focus on finding its own self. An Orientalist agenda is hard to miss in this endeavour because the non-West becomes just another category of study that nurtured Western Christian intellectualism.

3.   *Ecumenical Movement as Turn to World Christianity*

The turn to World Christianity gave an all together new perspective and paradigm to the existing discourse on Christianity. Paul Kollman states,

> We are moving—unevenly but steadily—"beyond the turn," where scholars of Christianity will be expected to consider the world or global implications of their work. To ignore such implications will place one's scholarship outside of an emerging consensus.[26]

The turn to World Christianity was rooted in the analysis of the demographic change in Christianity. The sweeping change in the demographic growth of Christianity in the southern hemisphere had already given a sign of a distinct Christianity which Walter Bühlmann envisioned, as early as 1977, as "Third Church."[27] This was later called as the emergence of World Christianity by Andrew Walls and Lamin Sanneh.[28]

However, one should take into serious consideration the debate how even the term World Christianity has conceived many problematics. For example, Namsoon Kang, critiquing Mark Noll's book *The New Shape of World Christianity: How American Experience reflects Global Faith,* argues that Noll reduces World Christianity to a code word for non-Western Christianity.[29] The binary of Western Christianity and non-Western Christianity is not questioned but implicitly confirmed. Another very important example could be of Dorottya Nagy's critical analysis of Sebastian Kim and Kirsteen Kim's usage of the term World Christianity in their work *Christianity as a World Religion.* Nagy criticises the book of containing territorial essentialism for it employs a geographical ordering of the continents.[30] A continent-based territorial division of World Christianity, like European Christianity, Asian Christianity, etc., is inherently problematic given the legacy of the ideas of European hegemony that went into the construction of territories.

Philip Jenkins' contribution, especially, in this aspect is much noteworthy. He asserts the fact that Christianity has been for centuries territorialised having the northern hemisphere as the centre of gravity and he highlights the "shift of the centre of gravity" to the south.[31] He sees this shift as "the most significant, and even the most revolutionary, in the contemporary world."[32] However, Jenkins places this 'shift' once again within a territorialised worldview. He locates the new Southern Christendom in contrast with the old Northern Christendom.[33] He draws the conclusion that "for the foreseeable future…the dominant current in emerging world Christianity is traditionalist, orthodox, and supernatural."[34] Therefore, he speaks about a "North-South cultural schism."[35] It appears that Jenkins maintains an almost ontological distinction between Western and non-Western Christianities by which he territorialises world Christianity. Therefore, there is a need to reimagine World Christianity as deterritorialising movements.

Reimagining Ecumenism as Deterritorialising Movements: Towards a Mission of the Multitude

The above problematisation of different imaginations of World Christianity tells us that there is a need for relocating World Christianity from an institutionalised rigid Christendom analogy to a more fluid and flexible movement perspective. Such a perspective enables to view World Christianity as a movement that advocates a radical deterritorialisation of Christianity. But it does not mean the exclusion of any one territory over the other. World Christianity might have a preferential choice for understudied themes and regions in the world, but it does not exclude the West or it does not place West and East or North and South in binary oppositions.[36] Rather it provides a space for 'different' and 'dissimilar' expressions of Christian belief beyond the binary of West and East. World Christianity, as a field of study, deliberately embraces the disorderliness of the lived forms of Christianity that take root and bear fruit in historical contexts of diverse peoples and dissimilar places on our earth. This is why Lamin Sanneh calls World Christianity as a movement of Christianity.

Sanneh's revisiting of World Christianity as movement is quite noteworthy. It advocates an alternative affirmation that is rooted in the spirit of movement challenging institutional Christendom, which essentialises the territorial nature of Christianity. Based on these assertions I would like to revisit the study of World Christianity and mission history for a deterritorialised world and towards a mission of the multitude.

Let me take here two important interventions to the study of World Christianity, especially in connection to the ecumenical history. One is from Dale Irvin, who says that the study of World Christianity is "particularly concerned with under-represented and marginalized communities of faith, resulting in a greater degree of attention being paid to Asian, African and Latin American experiences; the experience of marginalized communities within the North Atlantic world; and the experiences of women throughout the world."[37] And the other intervention is from Klaus Koschorke, who shares his discomfort with the existing curricula of World Christianity and

Mission History which he calls an outdated curricula, "which still reflect a rather limited Germanocentric, or at the best, Eurocentric perspective. Both in textbooks and in terms of academic organization, the world outside Europe is not really taken into account."[38] Though Irvin's statement emphasises the expressions of the marginal communities as the concern of World Christianity, it does reflect an essentialist territorial understanding of World Christianity. On the other hand Koschorke's genuine discomfort with the existing curricula of World Christianity has to be taken into serious consideration. But what concerns me most here is the territorialising world in binary opposition, namely, world inside Europe as the centre and world outside Europe as the margin.

We need to be cautious of falling into the trap of territorialising the centre and the margin, because it is the construction of the empire. As Kim Yong-Bok rightly said, contemporary theology cannot evade the context of empire.[39] Empire has become an all-embracing global order from where there is no escape. The relationship between empire and church is so complicated in the history of Christianity. Despite the illegitimate alliance with the empire through the ages, the church itself many a time had assumed role of a territorial institution and hierarchical agency. As Giorgio Agamben says, "Church had been an 'enclosed community' of authority and power."[40] Antonio Negri and Michel Hardt argue that there is an 'enclosed ontology' of the empire that controls, orders, and homogenises nations, people, cultures, etc. Agamben challenges the church to be a "coming community." For him, the church is "a community of those who have no community at all."[41] Here marginality becomes the core of Christianity. In other words, there is no marginal location outside of the being of the church. World Christianity, being a movement against life-erasing empires, should locate itself in the margins, because margins are salvific spaces of life-affirming spirituality. If we still assume margins as our 'exterior other' and by which we offer salvation to this marginal other, I think we inherit and embody the imperial 'enclosed ontology' in us. As Indian Christian theologian Y.T. Vinayaraj rightly asserts, margins are not our missiological other, or diaconal objects, rather they are the kenotic space in which we find salvation.[42]

Conclusion

The complex implications of *oikoumene* do invite from us a genuine and radical reimagination of implied meanings and definitions. The paradoxical notions of *oikoumene* within the biblical usages of the term, on the one hand, calls for a resistance of the imperial implications of the term and concept, and on the other hand, it also invites us to reclaim the anti-imperial implications of the term. Further, the important historical shifts in the theologies of *oikoumene* signifies the untameable and fluid nature of the idea and practice of ecumenism both in the history and in the present context. Such fluidity and flexibility invites us to reimagine a radical shift from the ecumenism of oneness to the ecumenism of manyness where multiplicity in the margins challenges the imperial notion of oneness. The celebration of manyness invites us to deterritorialise our histories and to challenge the grand narratives of our ecumenical past in order to let the multitude in the margins reshape the *oikoumene*.

Endnotes

[1] David E. Aune, "Revelation 1-5" in *World Biblical Commentary 52*, Dallas: Word, 1997, 228-239. However, there are scholars who challenge Aune's translation and interpretation. See for example, Barbara R. Rossing, " 'Alas for the Earth!' Lament and Resistance in Revelation 12," in *The Earth Bible*,

Vol. 5: *The Earth Story in the New Testament*, edited by Norman Habel and Shirley Wurth, Sheffield: Sheffield Academic Press, 2002, 183-195.

[2] Barbara R. Rossing, "(Re)claiming *Oikoumene?*, 84.

[3] Konrad Raiser, *Dictionary of the Ecumenical Movement*, edited by Nicholas Lossky et. al., Geneva: WCC, 2002, 1119.

[4] See, for example, Kaj Baago, *A History of the National Christian Council of India*, Nagpur: NCCI, 1965.

[5] The reports of the Missionary Conferences in Whitby (1947) and in New Delhi (1961) flood with such discussions.

[6] Jared Wicks presents a detailed study on the theological turn that took place in and after Vatican II that marked a huge shift in the theologies of ecumenism, especially in the Roman Catholic Church. See, Jared Wicks, *Investigating Vatican II: Its Theologians, Ecumenical Turn, and Biblical Commitment*, Washingdon, DC: Catholic University of America Press, 2018.

[7] Agnes Abuom, *Prospects and Challenges for Ecumenism and the Ecumenical Movement*, Address to the Swedish Ecumenical Weekend. https://www.oikoumene.org/en/resources/documents/executive-committee/uppsala-november-2018/prospects-and-challenges-for-ecumenism-and-the-ecumenical-movement, accessed on 18 February 2020.

[8] T. V. Philip, *Ecumenism in Asia*, Thiruvalla: ISPCK & CSS, 1994, 39.

[9] Konrad Raiser, *To be the Church*, Geneva: WCC, 1997, 39-40.

[10] Ibid., 41.

[11] "Policy Reference Committee II, Report 8.4, Appendix II: Globalization," in *Together on the Way: The Harare Report*, edited by D. Kessler, Geneva: World Council of Churches, 1998, 16.

[12] "Engaging Economic Globalization as a Communion," Geneva: Lutheran World Federation, 2001, 11.

[13] Barbara R. Rossing, "(Re)claiming *Oikoumene?*," 84.

[14] Vitor Westhelle, unpublished manuscript (Carnahan Lectures, ISEDET, Buenos Aires, Argentina; October 2001); as cited by Barbara R. Rossing, "(Re)claiming *Oikoumene?*," 84.

[15] WWC, *One World*, March-April 1991, 17.

[16] Michael Kinnamon, ed., *Signs of the Spirit: Official Report of the Seventh Assembly of the WCC, Canberra 1991*, Geneva: WCC, 1991, 173.

[17] Konrad Raiser, "Ecumenism in Search of a New Vision," in *The Ecumenical Movement: An Anthology of Key Texts and Voices*, edited by

Michael Kinnamon and Brian E. Cope, Geneva: WCC/Grand Rapids: Eerdmans, 1997, 73.

[18] Konrad Raiser, "Ecumenism in Search of a New Vision," 73.

[19] Marlene Perera, "New Models and New Praxis," in *Women's Visions*, edited by Ofelia Ortega, Geneva: WCC, 1995, 50-51; reprinted in *The Ecumenical Movement: An Anthology of Key Texts and Voices*, edited by Micael Kinnamon and Brian E. Cope, Geneva: WCC/Grand Rapids: Eerdmans, 1997), 248-249.

[20] Y.T. Vinayaraj, "Reconfiguring 'Christian Unity': Towards an Ecumenism of 'Manyness'" *Bangalore Theological Forum*, Vol. XLV, No. 2 (December 2013): 116-125; here, 121.

[21] S. Clarke, "World Christianity and Postcolonial Mission: A Path Forward for the Twenty-first Century," *Theology Today*, Vol. 71, No. 2, 2014: 192-206.

[22] See L. Newbigin, *Foolishness to the Greeks: Gospel and Western Culture*, Grand Rapids, MI: Eerdmans, 1986; *The Gospel in a Pluralist Society*, Geneva: WCC, 1989; *Truth to Tell: The Gospel as Public Truth*, Grand Rapids, MI: Eerdmans, 1991; and *The Open Secret: An Introduction to the Theology of Mission*, Grand Rapids, MI: Eerdmans, 1995.

[23] S. Clarke, "World Christianity and Postcolonial Mission," 192.

[24] https://www.ed.ac.uk/divinity/research/centres/world-christianity/about, accessed on 18.11.2018

[25] L. Sanneh, *Whose Religion is Christianity? The Gospel beyond the West*, Grand Rapids and Cambridge: William B. Eerdmans Publishing Company, 2003, 27-28.

[26] P. V. Kollman, "Understanding the World-Christian Turn in the History of Christianity and Theology," *Theology Today*, Vol. 71, No. 2, 2014: 164–177; here 166.

[27] W. Bühlmann, *The Coming of the Third Church: An Analysis of the Present and Future of the Church*, Maryknoll: Orbis Books, 1977.

[28] A. F. Walls and A. E. Akinade, *A New Day: Essays on World Christianity in Honor of Lamin Sanneh*, New York: Peter Lang, 2010; W. R. Burrows, M. R. Gornik, and J. A. McLean, *Understanding World Christianity: The Work and Vision of Andrew F. Walls*, Maryknoll: Orbis Books, 2011.

[29] Namsoon Kang, "Whose/Which World in World Christianity?: Toward World Christianity as Christianity of Worldly-Responsibility," in *A New Day: Essays on World Christianity in Honor of Lamin Sanneh*, edited by Andrew F. Walls and Akintunde E. Akinade, New York: Peter Lang, 2010, 37–38.

[30] D. Nagy, "Where Is China in World Christianity,"? *Diversities*, Vol. 12, No. 1, 2010: 70–83; here 74.

[31] P. Jenkins, *The Next Christendom. The Coming of Global Christianity*, New York: Oxford University Press, 2002, 1

[32] P. Jenkins, *The Next Christendom*, 1.

[33] P. Jenkins, *The Next Christendom*, 7.

[34] P. Jenkins, *The Next Christendom*, 8.

[35] P. Jenkins, *The Next Christendom*, 226.

[36] See the focus of the journal *Studies in World Christianity* expressed in its online portal: "The journal is concerned through its articles and book reviews to promote creative thinking and lively scholarly interchange in the interpretation of all aspects of Christianity as a world religion. Articles from historical, theological, and social scientific perspectives are equally welcome. Whilst the primary interest of the journal is in the rich diversity of Christian life and thought found in Africa, Asia, Latin America, Oceania, and eastern Europe, contributions that reflect on channels of influence in either direction between Christianity in the majority world and western Europe or North America will also be considered." https://www.euppublishing.com/loi/swc accessed on 23.11.2018

[37] D.T. Irvin, 'World Christianity: An Introduction', *The Journal of World Christianity*, Vol. 1, No. 1, 2008: 1.

[38] K. Koschorke, "New Maps of the History of World Christianity: Current Challenges and Future Perspectives," *Theology Today*, Vol. 71, No. 2, 2014: 178-191; here 180.

[39] K. Yong-Bok, "Asian Quest for Jesus in Global Empire," *Madang*, Vol.1, No.2, 2004:2.

[40] G. Agamben, *Coming Community*, trans. M. Hardt, Minneapolis: University of Minnesota Press, 1993, 1.

[41] G. Agamben, *Coming Community*, 1-2.

[42] Y. T. Vinayaraj, "Re-visiting 'the other': Towards a postmodern understanding of Christian mission." Retrieved from http://revytvinayaraj.blogspot.com/p/theology.html

Biblical Reflection I

Oikoumene
Community of Love
(Mark 1: 1-11, Genesis 18: 1-15,
II Corinthians 13:5-14)

Collect: Triune God, in whom we know the maker, see the saviour and experience the ever-abiding presence of the almighty, enable us to worship you in Spirit and truth. May your communion inspire us to transcend the barriers that divide us. Help us to build the communities of equals and *differents* where your love surpasses all things, through Jesus Christ our Lord, Amen!

The Russian artist and writer Vera Nazarian once said, "Love is made up of three unconditional properties in equal measure: acceptance, understanding and appreciation. Remove any one of the three and the triangle falls apart." It is the *tri-ness* or *many-ness* of love that makes love so inevitably imperative. The idea of a community of love, indeed, can never escape such a logic of manyness.

Mark 1:1-11

The faith of the early Christians in the *manyness* of the Godhead is well reflected in this pericope. John the Baptiser, God's 'path-straightener,' stands here as a witness to the *manyness* of God. The descending voice of God the parent and the descending act of the Holy Spirit are embodied in the ascending body of the Son, who was just *coming up* out of the water. This sight of triune revelation of God is surrounded by a socially significant sacrament: baptism. For John, baptism was a public demonstration of a new community, a community that has repented for its sins and now reformed and renewed by the incarnation of love. Jesus, the Son of God, stands here as the ultimate and supreme revelation of God's descending love. Thus a community that comes up out of the water and lives in differences and multiplicity is a community of love.

Genesis 18:1-15

The faith of the church in the *manyness* of God is traced back to the Abrahamic community of faith not just by the early Christian apologetics but also by contemporary theologians. The Mamre experience of Abraham and Sarah is remembered and reaffirmed as an experience of the triune God who is in loving communion with human beings. The unconditional hospitality of Abraham and Sarah to the *manyness* of Godhead is powerfully demonstrated in Abraham and Sarah's acceptance of the guests not as 'foreigners' but as part of their own self. They do not make any queries regarding the whereabouts of the 'guests', but get ready to cater to them unconditionally. An unconditional hospitality is not associated with right, law, debt or with duty. It is associated with mutual love, respect and being together for each other. In this act, Abraham and Sarah become part of a new community where Godhead is adored in its *manyness*. A pure gesture of love and hospitality becomes the foundation of such a new community.

II Corinthians 13:14

The communitarian benediction that the church has been affirming since centuries signifies that the church's faith is deeply rooted not in the *'oneness'* of her members but in their *manyness*. As God is perceived in God's *manyness*, the community of believers is also perceived in its foundational faith of being many in different identities. The plurality in God's image demands an acceptance of plurality in the image of humans too. It challenges the modernist stress on singularity and individuality. It is singularity and *oneness* that should be put to stake, and not plurality and *manyness*.

Ecumenism calls us to worship God who is diversified in *manyness* and who is different in God's own self, and to recreate communities which are so diverse, yet unified in the love of God. Love becomes a guiding principle to celebrate *manyness* and differences in human communities. Affirming God in *multiplicity* and *manyness* in the midst of hatred, injustice and turmoil thus is a daring act of faith and hope for a new community of love. Such a new community challenges all the singular claims of power and knowledge, transcends the barriers constructed by such claims and celebrates plurality and differences.

⌇

Biblical Reflection II

Oikoumene
Search for Divine Multiplicity
(Exodus 24: 12-18 and 32: 1-6)

The Good God and the Evil God met on the mountain top.
The Good God said, "Good day to you, brother."
The Evil God did not answer.
And the Good God said, "You are in a bad humour today."
"Yes," said the Evil God, "for of late I have been
often mistaken for you,
called by your name, and treated as if I were you,
and it ill-pleases me."
And the Good God said,
"But I too have been mistaken for you and called by your name."
The Evil God walked away cursing the stupidity of man.

Kahlil Gibran, *The Good God and The Living God*[1]

The struggle to choose between the Living God and the Ungod is as old as humankind. As Kahlil Gibran's poetic lines beautifully portray, humankind has often mistaken Living

God to Ungod. The selected text, when it is read in its entirety, is all about such a historical friction in the choice between Living God and Ungod. In other words, it is a living friction in the choice between the fluid, flexible and elastic experience of God and the static, fixed and rigid idea of God.

The first part of the read text is a very dramatic and spectacular screenplay that is believed to have been played on a high mountain stage which was called Sinai. The previous passage tells us that the people had seen the Lord. It was a theophany of the unfixable God—God's visible manifestation to the people. It was an experience of vibrant life that is manifested not in singularity, but in multiplicity. You can see that the elements of nature that appear in the text are all the symbol of life: Earth, Sky, Fire, Light, Air... everything.... They are all symbolising the multiplicity of the Living God. God's life in multiplicity is manifested in a spectacular way at Sinai. Interestingly, biblical scholars do not come to a conclusion about the exact geographical location of mount Sinai. That uncertainty gives us the gift of imagining Sinai as a fluid non-location-bounded space, as against the rigid and fixed Mount Zion. Reform Judaism even today believes that Sinai is a non-location-bounded space, in other words a borderless space/a non-bordered entity. That is why perhaps the diaspora Jews of Reform Judaism in different parts of the world imagine the idea of Temple Sinai. In that sense, Sinai is a borderless temple—it is a radical imagination of God's borderless dwelling. God cannot be static like an empire to be within the border. The theophany at Sinai manifests that God is borderless and beyond any fixity and singularity.

Now interestingly, while the borderless and manifold life of God was getting manifested at Sinai there was something extremely opposite happening underneath the mountain. What was that? The second part of our reading tells us that it was an act of border-building…. A border was erected by the lifeless forces, the forces of death, the forces of illusion, the forces of glittery imaginations…. In other words, an empire was getting built by the people of God. The making of the Golden Calf and the worship of an Ungod! Golden Calf as an empire!

Wait! Here we need to take a conscious break. Let us make a deliberate pause here and ask ourselves a few important questions: How can we possibly jump into the conclusion that the worship of the Golden Calf was sinful? Are we not proposing Yahweh worship as normative spirituality whereas the Golden Calf worship as deviant spirituality? In fact, the idea of the Golden Calf was borrowed from Canaanite spirituality. The spirituality of the occupied land and the people! The spirituality of the colonised! Are we not demonising an indigenous spirituality in our attempt to talk about the 'living God' of Israel? And if you read further in the same chapter 32, what happens to the Golden Calf worshippers is nothing but a genocide. Massacre of about 3,000 people on a single day! Bloodshed. Killing. In verse 27 onwards Moses says to the sons of Levi: "Put your sword on your side, each of you! Go back and forth from gate to gate throughout the camp, and each of you kill your brother, your friend, and your neighbour." The sons of Levi did as Moses commanded, and about 3,000 of the people fell on that day. Killed and massacred on that day. Their lives were taken away on that day. And Moses said, "Today you have ordained yourselves for the service of the LORD, each one at the cost of a son or a brother, and so have brought a blessing on yourselves this day." Does killing my brother, my sister, my son, my daughter, my neighbour bring blessing to me?

What an anarchic act it was! What a brutal belief! Are we justifying such a brutal genocide of about 3,000 people just because they had a 'different' spirituality? Is such bloodshed orchestrated by the living God? If yes, can such God be a living God? Do we need that God who takes pride and pleasure in bloodshed and genocide?

Well, let us come back from our deliberate break! Let us now consciously confess, what Israelites did on that day was not godly; it was brutally ungodly. The living God would never orchestrate such a brutal act of killing/genocide. Therefore, we need a different strand to read these scenes: On the one hand the spectacular scene of the theophany of the multiplicity of God at Sinai and on the other hand the ruthless, vicious, heartless scene of the genocide by the people of living God, a violent act of establishing an empire.

We must remember that the theophanies in the book of Exodus happen in the context of the empire. The immediate context of the people was the years-long suffering under the empire of Pharaoh. We may have to compare the earlier theophany at Mount Horeb in Exodus 3 with this Sinai theophany. We can see a huge shift in focus. In the Horeb theophany of Exodus 3 the focus was on liberation: "Let my people go." The theophany that led to the beginning of a liberation movement. But the focus of the theophany of our text is totally different; it is about the commandment!: "I will give you the tablets of stone, with the law and the commandment, which I have written for their instruction." Now we must ask, why does, after all, a liberated community need law, commandments and instruction? It tells us something very profound. It tells us that the liberated community was no longer a liberated community. It tells us about the prevalence of injustice within the liberated community. Therefore, the divine justice of liberation had to be replaced by the legal justice of the commandments. Remember, the commandments are the moral codes for the colonisers. Colonial history, history of empires, tells us that. It was a clear indication that Israel, the liberated community, was becoming an empire, a colonial power. When the liberation movement becomes a colonial power, such massacres do happen. In other words, when the multiplicity of the living God is not understood and embraced rightly, the massacre of the "other" in the name of singularity happens. Therefore, the making and worshipping of the Golden Calf must be understood as the sign of Israel's desire to be an empire. The worship of the Golden Calf was nothing but the fetishisation of religion and spirituality. It was the rejection of the God who is revealed in multiplicity and the celebration of the Ungod that demands singularity!

The history of Christianity is evident for the ungodly claims of singularity in the name of "One" God on the one hand and for the massacre of indigenous spirituality on the other. Sebastian Kappen, an Indian Jesuit theologian, says,

> Ungod is the God whom Christians fashioned to legitimize their lust for wealth and power. It is the Christian ungod who authorized the Christian kings to colonize and enslave all pagan nations and to exterminate indigenous tribes of Americas and the Pacific. It is the Christian ungod who permitted the Trans-Atlantic slave trade involving more than 30 million Africans. In short, the Christian ungod is a god who takes the side of the affluent and powerful against the vulnerable, a god with hands dripping with the blood of the innocent.[2]

Colonial Christianity often did not introduce the God of multiplicity manifested in the liberating Christ to the indigenous communities. Rather, it introduced *mono-God*, the colonial Christ. A voice from Africa unveils this historical truth very

80   Biblical Reflection II

powerfully. Vincent Gordon Harding, an African-American historian and social activist, describes the encounter of the enslaved Africans with the colonial Christ in these words:

> We first met this Christ on slave ships. We heard his name sung in praise while we died in our thousands, chained in stinking holds beneath the decks, locked in with terror and disease and sad memories of our families and homes. When we leaped from the decks to be seized by sharks we saw his name carved in the ship's solid sides. When our women were raped in the cabins, they must have noted the great and holy books on the shelves. Our introduction to this Christ was not propitious and the horrors continued on America's soil.[3]

Today we continue to experience the horrors of empires. And we also inherit such colonial horrors and scars on our bodies and minds in a colonial and postcolonial context like that of Asia and the Pacific. Colonial Christianity, though claimed to believe in the multiplicity of the living God, in reality did establish a singular and rigid notion of God by nullifying, erasing and massacring indigenous spiritualities. For Samoan novelist Albert Wendt, the Samoan indigenous spirituality was found in fluid humour and laughter and not in rigid commandments and laws. He argues that the rigid Christian morality was the ungod that colonial Christianity brought to the Pacific. He says,

> The missionaries (and all other puritans) brought pornography by instilling in us the bourgeois morality of Europe, making us ashamed of the very stories and situations which made us laugh. The puritan would have us believe that one does not exist below the navel. According to a poet friend, "The missionaries came with a Bible in one hand, and a chisel in the other." True Samoan humour went underground and remains there in those circles we call "respectable."[4]

The bourgeois morality of Europe, or call it Victorian morality, was the ungod that colonial Christianity used as a chisel to massacre indigenous spiritualities.

When we identify the ungods within and among us, we are challenged to reclaim the multiplicity of the living God that manifested on Mount Sinai, Mount Horeb and on the mount of transfiguration where Jesus embodied the multiplicity of the living God and continues to fight against all singular claims. The borderlessness of divine multiplicity must enable us to identify the bordering singularities within us and among us. We must strive to regain our ability to distinguish between the borderless God of life and the bordered ideas of God that is manifested in power, prosperity and the superiority of gender, race, ethnicity and spirituality. Our faith in the multiple life of God demands us to redeem our churches, our theologies, our spiritual practices from the worship of the single-truth. Our faith in God is a faith of reimagination. May we reimagine a decolonised borderless and multiple Christ who enables us to cherish the life in our indigenous spiritualities without compromising with the empires of our times. Let us experience the multiplicity of the living God today in our journey as an ecumenical community so that we may discard all single-strandic truth claims that we have been celebrating within our ecumenical endeavours. May God help us to that end. Let me conclude with yet another prose-poetry by Kahlil Gibran with a little variant:

"GARMENTS"

Upon a day Beauty (read Living God) and Ugliness (read Ungod) met on the shore of a sea. And they said to one another, "Let us bathe in the sea."

Then they disrobed and swam in the waters. And after a while the Ungod came back to shore and garmented himself with the garments of the Living God and walked away.

And the Living God too came out of the sea, and found not her raiment, and she was too shy to be naked, therefore she dressed herself with the raiment of the Ungod. And the Living God walked her way.

And to this very day men and women mistake the one for the other.

Yet some there are who have beheld the face of the Living God, and they know her notwithstanding her garments. And some there be who know the face of the Ungod, and the cloth conceals him not from their eyes.[5]

May the living God enable us to be *that someone* who cannot be deceived by the glittery garments of the Ungods of our time, Amen!

Endnotes

[1] Kahlil Gibran, *The Madman* in *The Complete Works of Kahlil Gibran*, New Delhi: Cross Land Books, 2015, 149.

[2] Sebastian Kappen, *Spirituality in the Age of Reconciliation*, Bangalore: Visthar, 1995, 3.

[3] Vincent Harding, "Black Power and the American Christ," in *The Black Power Revolt, edited by* Floyd Barbour, Boston: Beacon Press, 1969, 86.

[4] Cited in Tui Atua Tupua Tamasese Ta'isi Efi, "Whispers and Vanities in Samoan Indigenous Religious Culture," in *Whispers and Vanities: Samoan Indigenous Knowledge and Religion*, edited by Tamasailau M. Suaalii-Sauni... (et.al.), Wellington: New Zealand Huia Publishers, 2014.

[5] Kahlil Gibran, *The Wanderer* in *The Complete Works of Kahlil Gibran*, New Delhi: Cross Land Books, 2015, 51-52.

Biblical Reflection III

Oikoumene of the Empire vs *Oikoumene* of God

The opposite of faith is not unfaith but the fear of affirming the ambiguity of our faith at a fearful time, and the challenge for the followers of Christ is to transcend fear even at a fearful time. This invites us not to be phobic even when we are seized by terror of the empire. Today the identity of the religious minorities around the world is under threat. The very existence of minorities is seized by terror of the empire. The faith and freedom of these communities are disturbed. Therefore, one needs to ask the pertinent question repeatedly, what does it mean to affirm our faith in freedom in the midst of the reality of hatred, intolerance and violence? How does the church, as *oikoumene*, the household of God, boldly affirm the reality that is fear-ridden and full of ambiguity?

Mark 16:08—"So they (women) went out and fled from the tomb, for terror and amazement had seized them; and they said nothing to anyone, for they were afraid." These women whom Mark lists among the multitude were aware of the ambiguity of their faith. This awareness enabled them to transcend fear even at a fearful time and to become witnesses to the Risen Lord, the counter to the empire. These women were chosen to pass on the good news of freedom. They were seized by terror, a very obvious emotional state of the *margins*. They did not pretend to be otherwise. Ambiguity of their faith was affirmed and thus they became the channels of God's irreversible freedom—freedom from empire, the empire that waged a war of conspiracy to seize the multiple truths and diverse life-experiences of the multitude, in the name of *oneness* of the empire. Mark very impressively discerns the imperial signs of his times and propagates an alternative expression of faith through Jesus, the crucified and the risen.

Keeping this insight in mind, let us explore the Gospel of Mark to converse with the similar signs of our times. Let us together raise a few issues:

1. The challenge of empire, both in the time of Mark and in our time. What is to be our response, as an ecumenical community of faithful, to the empire of our time?

2. The locatedness of the people of faith, the multitude and the people who caused fear in the lives of the multitude. Where do we stand?

3. Jesus between multitudes and empire. How are we challenged by Jesus?

1.   The Challenge of the Imperial *Oikoumene*

Scholars generally agree that Mark's Gospel account is the earliest of the three Synoptic Gospels. Mark seems to have written his account sometime between 64 CE, the end of the persecution under Nero, and 75 CE, before Mathew and Luke wrote their Gospel accounts. It was a time of tension between the Christian church and the Roman Empire. It was a time when Rome wanted to establish its *oikoumene* by massacring the manyness lived by the multitude in the margins. It was in such a context that Jesus proclaims the *oikoumene* of God, which is full of diversities and multiplicities, as an alternative.

The reality and terror of the empire was prominent when Mark wrote his Gospel account. It was indeed a fearful time. In this situation Mark calls for a form of costly discipleship that should break through, confront and even transcend the reality of the fear of the empire.

In taking this position Mark reflects what Jesus would have meant in speaking of the *basileia* of God. It was a direct confrontation of the Empire of Rome and therefore Jesus' alternative was the *oikoumene* of God. Jesus deliberately took a political concept to express 'the good news' of freedom that spoke of an alternative *oikoumene*. This alternative oikoumene of God invited the multitude, the people of faith who were filled with fear, and offered them a different kind of peace that guaranteed freedom of proclamation, in other words, freedom of confessing and professing an alternative belief.

In our time today the predominant challenge is the reality of empire. The imperial power of neocolonialism through transnational power networks are attempting to reorder the world. 'Fear' occupies a significant place in the everyday reality of the people in the margins. In this situation we too feel helpless like the 'ochlos', the multitude, the sheep without a shepherd—to whom Jesus held out the promise of the *oikoumene* of God as an alternative. We are in a situation of crisis that calls for a change in perspective—an epistemological shift—and its consequent praxis. In the face of empire we are called to make a shift by following the way of the suffering servant who proclaimed the *oikoumene* of God as an alternative that holds out the promise of freedom for all: that includes freedom of religion/belief, freedom of speech and freedom of reclaiming one's own alternative power.

2. The Locatedness of the Legitimate Members of the *Oikoumene*

Now, the second issue we need to raise is: how Mark locates the idea of freedom promised to the multitudes, the people of faith at a fearful time. Mark uses two sets of characters to set this out. On the one hand there are Jewish and Gentile authorities. They have status, power and security but are essentially insecure. They are afraid, because their authority and power are not necessarily legitimate. They are the tenants of the vineyard who are even willing to kill the son and heir to keep what they have wrongfully acquired (12:1-12). They will do anything to protect their self-interest. In their effort to protect themselves they are always in fear.

The religious and political authorities in Mark show fear (12:12). They were afraid of Jesus and the multitude. They were afraid of Jesus because he was popular with the multitude, and he spoke of what the people knew to be true but were afraid to say to the face of the powers that be.

On the other side are the ordinary people, the *ochlos*, the multitude. Mark makes a very creative use of this term. It is interesting that he avoids the term *laos* used very frequently by the Greek Jewish Bible, the Septuagint. 'Laos' occurs only twice in Mark: in 7:6, which is a quotation from the Old Testament, and in 14:2, as uttered by the Jewish authorities.

Why does Mark prefer the term *ochlos*? In CE 70, with the fall of Jerusalem and the persecution in Israel, people had lost their identity and were driven as sheep without a shepherd. As the *ochlos* begin to take shape in Mark, certain characteristics begin to appear. Unlike the authorities, who are too selfish, self-centred and self-righteous, the *ochlos* make enormous attempts to help others. They bring a paralytic to be cured by Jesus (2:3). They bring a hearing and speech impaired man and beg Jesus to cure him (7:32). They bring a blind man and beg Jesus to touch him (8:22). This is the essence of the alternative *oikoumene*, an all-inclusive and just household.

Here, Mark establishes an idea of commonwealth among the multitude. Through the notion of 'life in common,' Mark proposes a political project of the multitude to initiate an ethics of democratic political action within and against empire. It is a democracy that invites everyone to share and participate in the commonwealth. In fact, the true essence of *ekklesia*. This fosters the capacity to live the countless voices, and especially with the dispersed multiplicity of non-voices and non-identities. Through this, Mark proposes an ethics of freedom for living in our common world and articulates a possible constitution for radical democracy in the context of empire. To fight against empire is to search for a life in common. *Oikoumne* is all about that. Coming together, *koinonia*, celebration of life in communion and all these are the foundation of the *oikoumene* of God and the multitude, the legitimate members of the *oikoumene*.

3. Jesus the Cornerstone of *Oikoumene*

Third issue—Jesus between multitude and empire. Jesus stands here as the Messiah of the multitude. In proclaiming the 'Empire of God,' Jesus opened up avenues of hope for the multitude. But for Rome that was sedition. The life of Jesus was under threat for this reason. Yet he took the side of the powerless multitude. He proclaimed and prophesied the fall of the empire, and demanded the freedom of the multitude to profess their faith even at a fearful time.

Mark 13:14-23—Mark uses an apocalyptic language borrowed from the Jewish Bible, especially from Daniel and Maccabeus. In the context of war, hatred, intolerance and violence, the apocalyptic language was used as a powerful mechanism to counter the empires. Mark in his own context of intolerant empire uses this language and presents Jesus within a political agitation. The words of Jesus in 13:14—"when you see the desolating sacrilege set up where it ought not to be"—and the Markan commentary to it—"let the reader understand"— should be understood within such a sociopolitical struggle. What does desolating sacrilege mean here? For Daniel, it referred to Antioches Epiphanes IV. Epiphanes, the Hellenistic Greek emperor, attacked Jerusalem in 168 BCE. And in Mark it refers to the Roman Empire. Jesus, discerning the signs of his times, invites the multitude that followed him to react to the empire, and demands not to stand passive. Desolating sacrilege is the threat to the freedom of the multitudes to live in manyness. As a globalising empire it demands homogeneity from the multitude. Whereas Jesus stands here as the cornerstone of God's *oikoumene* which embraces and celebrates multiplicity and heterogeneity.

Jesus did not stand on the side of the empire that threatened the very life of the multitude. Rather, he stood by the side of the common people. Verses 15, 16, 17—the ones on the housetop, the ones in the field striving hard for his daily bread, the one who is pregnant and dreaming of the future of her offspring— they are the concern of Jesus. Here the invitation of Jesus to flee does not demand a mechanism of escapism, rather he invites the multitude not to surrender to the power of the empire at any cost. Mark demands his readers to contextualise their faith by using such an apocalyptic language and hence it should demand our attention to the universal contextuality of it.

Hans Weber, a German biblical scholar, equalises the metaphor of *desolating sacrilege* to the empire of Hitler and draws the implication that it was an invitation of Jesus to the Jews in Germany during the time of Hitler to flee and not to surrender to the empire. Today we need to ask who or what that *desolating sacrilege* in our context is. We may have to see the growing neocolonial empires of our time as the *desolating sacrilege* which threatens the manyness of the multitude. The fascist empires in different parts of the world attempt to erase the beauty of being different by inscribing *oneness* on the docile and fragile bodies of the multitude today. Jesus cautions us from falling into the trap of either being phobic of the Other in a multireligious context or of being occupied by the forces of homogenising empires.

In our context of growing power of neocolonialism we need an epistemological shift to understand the gravity of the multifaceted network of the empire. The neocolonial empire is a network of power that includes political ideologies, dominant transnational institutions, capitalist corporations and other powers. In this imperial network of power, not all powers are equal, yet they maintain the order intact so as to keep their positions within. Empire exists by creating conflicts and violence both within and outside. Such conflicts are not exclusively 'political' but loop within and beyond sociocultural boundaries, producing and reproducing a docile multitude. This is where Jesus becomes the new hope for a shared living. *Oikoumene* of God is all about sharing and celebrating in mutuality.

Church is the community of *ochlos*, like those women near the tomb, utterly powerless in the context of hate, murder, violence and threats. But we are invited to believe that the risen Lord is still with us, with the *ochlos* enabling us to continue resisting the empire. We are challenged not to be phobic of the 'other' but to be the powerful witnesses of God's transcendental freedom. We are invited to affirm a necessary ambiguity of our faith, avoiding absolutist claims of rationality. It is in ambiguity and complexity we resist against all the absolutist claims of the empire. And in such ambiguities alone we may be able to affirm our faith in God beyond our Christian worldview and to include our common "Other" with whom we are ought to establish an *oikoumene* of relationship.

Liturgy I

Celebrating the *Oikoumene* of God

Locating the Context and the Content of Worship

Oikoumene of the Empire

We speak of Empire, because we discern a coming together of economic, cultural, political and military power in our world today, that constitutes a reality and a spirit of lordless domination, created by humankind yet enslaving simultaneously; an all-encompassing global reality serving, protecting and defending the interests of powerful corporations, nations, elites and privileged people, while imperiously excluding even sacrificing humanity and exploiting creation; a pervasive spirit of destructive self-interest, even greed—the worship of money, goods and possessions; the gospel of consumerism, proclaimed through powerful propaganda and religiously justified, believed and followed; the colonization of consciousness, values and notions of human life by the imperial logic; a spirit lacking in compassionate justice and showing contemptuous disregard for the gifts of creation and the household of life.

CWM Theology Statement 2010

Empire displays strong tendencies to domesticate Christ and anything else that poses a challenge to its powers. Christ becomes part of the system to such a degree that little or no room exists for the pursuit of alternative realities of Christ.

Joerg Rieger

Preparation: Worshippers may gather in a circle (in case of a huge gathering, multiple circles within the circles may be formed). The floor may be decorated with varieties of flowers, fruits, plants and colourful pieces of cloth symbolising the multiplicity of life. Each participant will bring something distinct from her/his own context (be it a handful of soil, a flower, a stone, a piece of cloth, a leaf, a pen, a fruit, a chocolate, etc.) to share with another member of the *oikoumene* as a sign of 'gift of life'.

Welcome: Worshippers welcome each other by sharing their 'gifts of life'. After the sharing of gifts all will say in unison:

This I share with you, dear sojourner, as a sign of our collective journey in this fragile **oikoumene.** *This gift may sing to you the saga of our constant combat with the empire. May this _____ (you may name your gift here) tell you the story of my struggle with the innumerable empires around me, the way it provokes me, lures my being, hurts my emotions, and deceits my consciousness. May it also tell you how I dearly dare to challenge the empire by defeating its ever-haunting claims on the vulnerable lives of many like me. Does it also not tell you, how shamelessly I try to be one of them, the inducement to become an empire?*

Thank you for your gift, dear housemate in God's oikoumene. *Yes, I do hear your songs and stories of struggle with an imperial* oikoumene. *How good it is to come together to our eternal refuge from whom nothing is hidden. Let us worship God for in God we have wisdom and strength to face the empires that invade the* oikoumene *of love, justice and peace.*

Invocation

(Three representatives belonging to different church traditions come to the middle of the circle and light a candle, a lamp and a torch and lead the following prayers respectively.)

God of multiplicity, the breath of life, provider of love and hope, we worship you in your borderless *oikoumene*. You created us with beauty and wisdom, with courage and conscience, with strength and vulnerability. We rejoice in your being that is manifested in plurality and diversity.

We find peace and joy in your *oikoumene*, O God of all creation!

Jesus, the cornerstone of God's *oikoumene*, you fought for those who were forcefully and conveniently excluded from God's household. It is under your cross that we are reconciled with God and God's creation. We look at you for the power to dare to challenge the empires of our time that extinguish the beauty of manyness.

We find our refuge in your all-embracing arms, O our Redeemer!

Holy Spirit, the creative energy of life, you breathe in us the breath of diversity. You wake us up from our deep sleep in the face of suppression of multiplicity and mutuality. We long for the storm that you blow to unchain our bonded spirits and bodies. And you rekindle in us the spirit of togetherness celebrating our differences.

We find strength and courage in your untameable power, O our Helper!

Holy Trinity, whose nature is mutuality, multiplicity and ecumenicity, in your name we come together to share, to love and to be loved, to learn and to teach, to challenge and to be challenged by each other in our journey towards God's *oikoumene.*

We praise and adore you, God of love and justice, Amen!

Hymn: For Christ and the Church (The following hymn or any vernacular hymn that fits can be sung)

1. "For Christ and the Church" we stand
   United heart and hand;
   Our lips His praise to speak,
   Our hands to help the weak;
   Our feet the lost to seek,
   "For Christ and the Church."

   > *Refrain:*
   > "For Christ and the Church" we stand,
   > United heart and hand;
   > Our lives henceforth we give to live
   > "For Christ and the Church."

2. "For Christ and the Church" we pray,
   And labour day by day;

With zeal and courage new
We'll strive some work to do,
And keep our cov'nant true,
"For Christ and the Church." [Refrain]

3. "For Christ and the Church" we sing,
   And glad hosannas bring;
   Since He hath made us free,
   And promised victory,
   Our motto still shall be,
   "For Christ and the Church." [Refrain]

Confession

Representative 1: "My way of worship was the only right way of worship," so I thought for a long time, without knowing that I was worshiping an 'ungod' that tormented me with a spirit of pride and exclusivism. Like me, many of you might have misunderstood God's desire of keeping us united. We thought, miserably wrong, that being united costs us our diversities and multiplicities. We failed to understand that God created us diverse and different and that God found it good. Let us confess our sins of ignorance and misinterpretation of God's *oikoumene*.

God, we ask for your forgiveness for our imperial notions of *oikoumene*

Representative 2: Even though I have been part of the ecumenical movement for decades now, I have failed to see it as a people's movement. As a result, I have not embodied God's *oikoumene* that requires from me an integral involvement with the people in the margins. Like me, many of you might have enjoyed ecumenical fellowships for sheer selfish privileges and thus overlooked the true spirit of *oikoumene* that our ancestors, especially in the Global South, embodied. Let us confess of our sins of celebrating our privileges in the name of the ecumenical movement and not living the ecumenism.

God, we ask for your forgiveness for not embodying ecumenical movement as people's movement.

Merciful God, we come to your presence in repentance. Forgive us Lord for our iniquities, for our arrogance, for our occupying nature, for our enslaving behaviours, for our desire to be the empires, for fetishising our spiritualities with ghettoed denominationalism. We admit that our souls are sickened by the sense of pride. We have othered our fellow beings in the name of race, gender, territorial superiority and so on. We confess that we have failed to identify your voice in the 'different' spiritual expressions of our fellow humans and creation. Forgive us Lord, for being the devotees of ungods. Cleanse our bodies and minds, O God, in your sanctuary of *oikoumene*. Take us to the non-location-bounded mountaintop so that we may be able to see the depth of your Life. Make us once again the disciples of the living God to embark an unending journey towards freedom, dismantling the pyramids of systemic sin and evil. In the name of our co-pilgrim Jesus Christ, the borderless ecumenical manifestation, we pray, Amen.

Readings from the Scripture
(In between each readings a vernacular Bhajan/Song/Hymn may be sung)

Narratives of Ecumenical Journey
(Two or three representatives from the community would share their experiences of ecumenical journey)

Sermon/Dialogue/Collective Reflections

Song: A relevant song based on the sermon/reflection/dialogue may be sung

Affirmation of Faith
We believe in God the creator, sustainer and protector, who made the creation diverse and distinct *oikoumene.*

We believe in Jesus Christ, our saviour and liberator. He is the expression of God's redeeming love, the mark of humanness, source of courage, power and love. He is the ground of God's *oikoumene.*

We believe that God through Jesus Christ resides among us with the waters, the creatures both inside the water and outside. God suffers not only our powerlessness but also our divisions. God desires to unite us all, but with all our diversities and differences celebrated.

We believe that through death and resurrection God gives life and dignity with all its multiplicity. God provides us the opportunity to celebrate our distinctiveness in unity. We believe that God calls us to take part as an ecumenical community in God's mission of challenging the empires of our time and promising hope to those in despair.

We believe that the Holy Spirit revives our bodies, minds and souls. Our defeated and broken spirits are uplifted by the Holy Spirit preparing us to combat with the empires of this world and to rebuild God's *oikoumene* that promises love, peace and beauty for all. Amen

Intercessory Prayer

(Representatives from various church traditions may offer the following prayers, preferably translated to their regional languages.)

God of diversity and multiplicity, we pray for a renewed understanding of unity among the churches of various traditions that they may come together without dismantling their distinctive Christian heritage.

Hear our prayer, O God

We pray for a salvific solidarity among different churches for the people whose lives are threatened by the empires of our time. We pray that the churches come together to fight against the evil of various forms of imperialism and colonisation to have a better cooperation so that in our unity we may work for justice both outside and within the empire.

Hear our prayer, O God

We pray for the freedom of people and regions that are still under colonial and neocolonial occupation. We pray that those people's fight for liberation may bring them victory at the earliest and end colonialism and related oppression.

Hear our prayer, O God

We pray for the ecumenical movement and for all who suffer, pray and toil in the cause of unity and justice: that all these efforts may bear good fruits to the honour and glory of your most holy name.

Hear our prayer, O God

We pray for fresh insight that we might find alternatives to empire and injustice. Renew our commitment and challenge our assumptions as we pray the prayer Jesus taught us, in a new way (A prayer adopted from the WSCF's Universal Day of Prayer 2016 Liturgy):

Eternal Spirit,
Earth-maker, Pain-bearer, Life-giver,
Source of all that is and that shall be,
Father and Mother of us all,
Loving God in whom is heaven:
The hallowing of your name echo through the universe!
The way of your justice be followed by the peoples of the world!
Your heavenly will be done by all created beings!
Your commonwealth of peace and freedom sustain our hope
and come on earth.
With the bread we need for today, feed us.
In the hurts we absorb from one another, forgive us.
In times of temptation and test, strengthen us.
From trials too great to endure, spare us.
From the grip of all that is evil, free us.
For you reign in the glory of the power that is love,
now and for ever, Amen.

Closing Hymn/Song/Bhajan: *TU HI DATA VISHWA VIDHATHA* (SCM Ecumenical Anthem) Or any English or regional songs may be sung

Going Out
(All hold each other's hand and say together):

Together we go, together we grow, together we witness our spirit of ecumenism in challenging the *oikoumene* of the empire, and reliving our diversities, multiplicities and manyness. May the triune God be with us now and forever more, Amen.

Liturgy II

Oikoumene:
The Household of Nonconformism

Locating the Context and the Content of Worship

Fascism, Communalism and Colonialism

Churches around the globe witness a sturdy growth in fascist, communal and hypernational colonialism. Fascism stands firmly on the logic of oneness that wages a war against celebrating manyness. The very notion of being different is challenged and demonised by the homogenising forces of fascism. Ecumenism, as a faith expression of manyness, must contest the legitimacy of fascism and affirm the freedom of being different and the freedom of dissent.

"The strategic adversary is fascism... the fascism in us all, in our heads and in our everyday behaviour, the fascism that causes us to love power, to desire the very thing that dominates and exploits us."

Michel Foucault

"The hope of a secure and livable world lies with disciplined nonconformists who are dedicated to justice, peace and brotherhood."

Martin Luther King, Jr

Preparation: The worship area will be placed with several visible symbols as metaphor of fascist colonialism and also of people's collective noncomformist protest against fascism and celebration of dissent and being different. For example:

- Chairs upside down, symbolising the hope of the ecumenical community in the fall of fascism.

- Baptismal Font upside down, symbolising, on the one hand, people's dissent against being baptised by the fascist empire and, on the other hand, as a metaphor for the fascist nature of the church.

- Eucharist elements (preferably alternative elements as against the traditional wafers and wine) may be covered with colourful and shabby cloths, symbolising the multitude's dissent against homogenising the divine and noncomformism towards the fascist notion of purity and pollution.

Invocation

Drums will be beaten as the worshippers gather together (Indigenous dance or singing may also be used) denoting the vibrancy and radicality of our spirits that cannot be controlled and tamed by any fascist forces of our time.

Representative 1 recites the Bible Verse:

"God makes wars cease to the end of the earth; God breaks the bow, and shatters the spear; God burns the shields with fire." (Psalm 46:9)

Response: We believe that God shatters the dreams of the empires that try to massacre our beauty of manyness by imposing their weapon of oneness on us. We worship you, O God of difference and diversity.

Representative 2 recites the Bible Verse:
"Why are you looking among the dead for one who is alive? He is not here; he has been raised." (Luke 24:5-6)

Response: We believe that Jesus Christ is not among the forces of death and darkness; He lives in the colourful world of the multitude celebrating life in multiplicity. We worship you, O God of multiple colours.

Representative 3 recites the Bible Verse:
"All of them were filled with the Holy Spirit and began to speak in other languages, as the Spirit gave them ability." (Acts 2:4)

Response: We believe that the Holy Spirit is the expression of divine multiplicity and manyness. The Holy Spirit gives us the courage to daringly voice our dissent and nonconformism in the face of fascist imposition of oneness. We worship you, O God of courage and strength. Amen.

A dance may be performed while a hymn/song of praise is sung, representing the harmonious symphony of our gifts of being different.

Confession (Together):
God of justice, our hearts are heavy
with pain and suffering of the ages,
with the crusades and the holocausts,
with the genocides and the ethnic 'cleansings'
with the 'disciplining' of the docile bodies and minds

with the 'normalising' of different sexualities
of thousands and thousands of years
The blood of the victims is still warm,
The cries of anguish still fill the nights.
Unto you we lift up our outspread hands

We thirst for your mercy and forgiveness, O God.

God of courage, our hearts are heavy
with our failures to be your image
with our unwillingness to be the darers
with the guilt of conforming to fascist forces
with the fear of embracing the 'other'
with the fascination for homogeneous life
of thousands and thousands of years
The blood of the victims is still warm,
The cries of anguish still fill the nights.
Unto you we lift up our outspread hands

We thirst for your mercy and forgiveness, O God.

Forgive and Empower us O Lord, to be darers, dissenters and nonconformists in the face of fascism, communalism and colonialism. Amen.

A Representative reads the Bible verse:
Jesus was left alone with the woman, who remained standing there.

He looked up and said, "Woman, where are they? Has no one condemned you?"

"No one, Sir," she replied.

"Neither do I condemn you," said Jesus, "go away, and don't sin anymore."

Readings from the Bible (including one from a non-canonised book)
(The Scriptures may be read in different languages)

Watching of a documentary/video that reflect the episodes of brutality of the fascist empires of our time and also the biopics of those who remained nonconformists even at the cost of their own lives.

An open conversation engaging with the Scriptures and the incidents screened.

Song or cultural performance reflecting the theme

Prayer of Commitment and Lord's Prayer (Inspired by the WSCF-UDPS Liturgy for 2019)

Representative 1:	God of heavens and earth
	We lift up our hearts in courage
	To give thanks and praise
	To the God of Justice and Beauty
	To recommit our being
	To resist the evil of fascist colonialism
	And to be darers, dissenters and nonconformists
All:	**So that together, we can say;**
	Hallowed be your name
Representative 2:	Give us the wisdom

To come together
To celebrate our differences
To embrace the 'unlike'
And to challenge fascism
With a spirit of unity in diversity

All: **So that together, we can say;**
Your kingdom come,
Your will be done, on earth as in heaven

Representative 3:   Challenge and inspire us
To share our gifts in mutuality
To empty the unjust wealth of the empire
To be hospitable to all
And to embrace "strangers"

All: **So that together, we can say;**
Give us today our daily bread

Representative 4:   Give us the daring
To question the fascist empire
To be self-reflexive
To learn from the other
And to rejoice in your image in others

All: **So that together, we can say;**
Forgive us our sins
As we forgive those who sin against us
Lead us not into temptation
But deliver us from evil.

Representative 5:   May we know the image of God
That is manifested in diversity

May we grow in the likeness of Christ,
who is a revolutionary dissenter
And be open to the nonconformist Spirit

All: **For yours is the reign, the power
and the glory
Now and forever more.
Amen**

Closing Hymn/Song/Bhajan/Chanting

Going Out

Let us go out with courage and strength to defeat fascism, communalism and colonialism. May the dissenter Jesus guide us on our way.

Let us dare to be nonconformists disturbing and challenging the forces that erase manyness. May the Holy Spirit sustain us in this journey of a radical revolution.

Let us joyfully celebrate our differences and thus dare to irk the empires of oneness and thus defeat them for a better future. May God be with us forever and ever, Amen!

Courage to Be DARERS
De- and Re-construct Ecumenism

Jooseop Keum[*]

The rapidly changing realities of the world and of Christian presence necessitate the need to reimagine ecumenism in ways that it adequately presents itself as a spiritual and moral force, an agent of change for a new world of justice, peace and life for all. This seems all the more necessary because, in recent times, on account of a variety of factors both ecumenism and the ecumenical movement seem to have increasingly become uninspiring and ineffective. A group of young theologians who gathered together as an International Theological Colloquium for Transformative Ecumenism reflected as follows: "The ecumenical movement is in crisis—a deep crisis painfully felt everywhere. It is a crisis brought by a prophetic bankruptcy in terms of the movement, an intellectual bankruptcy in terms of the ecumenical spirit and vision, and a moral bankruptcy in terms of the leadership." The ecumenical movement is no longer strongly rooted in the people and it does not speak a prophetic voice which echoes in the realities of people's struggles for life. The ecumenical movement no longer produces a new and heart-beating vision for the church and the world that are deeply divided and wounded. The ecumenical leadership has suffered from bureaucratic and business-oriented mindedness that lacks the sense of calling and devotion.

It is painful to listen to the criticisms of younger theologians. But there is a proverb in Korea, "A good medicine is bitter." I believe that this book is a bitter but a good prescription to the modern ecumenical movement. In my view, the prescription suggests the following seven treatments for future ecumenism. 1) Shifting the centre of ecumenism from the Eurocentric to World Christianity. 2) Relocating from an international eclecticism to a people-centred grassroots approach. 3) Revisioning beyond an institutionalism to a movement orientation. 4) Rebuilding foundations of ecumenism from doctrinal to spirituality. 5) Discovering ecumenism from the margins. 6) New Ecumenism affirming diversity. 7) Ecumenical discipleship based on faith not politics. These seven topics should be continuously researched so that an authentic ecumenism that is relevant to the contemporary world may emerge from the Christian mission and movement in the Global South. In order to do so, we DARE to challenge the current ecumenical discourse of empire!

Oikoumene is a vision that took shape as a movement of churches amidst division and strife in the world, asserting that we, human beings and all living beings on the earth, belong to one household of God. As a response to our Lord's prayer "that they all may be one" (John 17:11), the goal of Christian unity was seen and pursued as a precursor to the realisation of the vision of grand reconciliation of all people and beings in God (Eph.1:10). The purpose and scope of Christian understanding of unity have been constantly evolving, to include the unity of humankind and the whole of creation. Since we are living in a troubled and broken world and facing internal challenges within, the ecumenical movement should reimagine its vision and rejuvenate it.

Transforming Ecumenism to Rejuvenate Movement

The unity given by the triune God moves on common witness, mission, evangelism, service and justice and peace. Constant efforts have been made by the ecumenical movement to realise this unity by staying together, growing together and moving together. It is inevitable that we develop institutions as a means of trying to secure the integrity of the movement. However, over time the institution can lose the vision for the movement and fall into the temptation to only serve its self-interest. In such a situation, it is vital to reimagine ecumenism at this particular juncture of history and the context of the ecumenical movement. Therefore, we need to introduce a process to reimagine ecumenism through "transforming together." It is not a mere theological orientation but a spirituality of life that inspires the pilgrimage of transformation in an attitude of humility and openness to the presence and work of the Spirit in obedience to Jesus' new commandment to love God and neighbours as ourselves (Jn.13:34; Lk. 10: 25-37). It will strive to protect and safeguard the integrity of creation in resisting the schemes and strategies of the powerful for unlimited greed of economic growth and benefits that caused a COVID-19 world.

Ecumenical Vocation and Spirituality

The troubles we experience today affect a wide range of human experience on the individual, community and world level as well as the whole of creation. Our relationship with ourselves, our communities and even the earth are undergoing a profound and unprecedented crisis. In our globalised world, ecumenical spirituality and worship can provide one of the greatest sources of hope for healing these broken relationships. This challenge demands the help/gift of the life-giving Spirit of God, who can safely guide us. In a fragmenting and exclusionary world, transforming ecumenism asserts the essential mutuality and interdependence of all that God created and continues to create. Affirming that diversity is God's self-expression, it seeks to be inclusive and respectful of all that God wills for the people of the earth. It, therefore, confronts and transforms all faith traditions, cultures, ideologies and systems that perpetrate the notion of the 'other,' holding some as inferior, unworthy and expendable. It is, therefore, a spiritual choice, an attitude and vocation that embraces God's plan of salvation in Jesus Christ confronting and transforming attitudes and values, and options and actions that defy God's purposes for life both at personal and larger levels. Such a spirituality compels us to give an account of our hope through actions and initiatives that offer creative alternatives. Jesus not only condemned those who were unjust and oppressive but also, through his teachings and actions, proposed possibilities that nurture the seeds of God's reign. Therefore, ecumenical formation should receive fresh priorities to meet the future of the ecumenical movement and vocation. More spiritually based, mission-oriented and contextually equipped curriculum should be developed.

Dialogue Embracing the Future

Religious fundamentalism is rising all over the world and in all religions today. It serves as an "emperor's cloth," as an ideological backbone of political fascism, racism and other forms of exclusive claims. The ecumenical movement should strongly uphold interfaith dialogue to make ourselves and other religious people to be open to dialogue. Religion which is not 'dialogue-able' is not a good news but a bad news to people. Therefore, the ecumenical interfaith dialogue should go beyond intellectual discipline or diplomatic gestures. Fighting together against violent extremism has to be an urgent common task of all the parties in the interreligious dialogue for our peaceful coexistence. We have to intentionally create a space to encourage open and moderate religious leaders and people to be in the mainstream in our attitude and relationship with other religions. Meanwhile, ecumenical dialogues were never limited to interfaith dialogue. Dialogue with secular ideologies, science and cultures enriched and widened the ecumenical movement in the past. As we will face a revolutionary change of human life due to rapid scientific and technical advancement, the so-called 4th Industrial Revolution, a dialogue with science and technology is an imperative to embrace the future in the ecumenical movement. The contemporary information technology and biotechnology developments of the 4th Industrial Revolution have unleashed Cyber-Physical Systems that are impacting human life and identity, and this has major implications for future ecumenical relations and engagement. In the coming era of trans-humanism and Artificial Intelligence (AI) robots, ecumenical ethical engagement at the strategic level of policy formulation and technological design are very necessary to ensure accountability for those actors who are setting the agenda and reaping the profits for the advance of technology.

Youth at the Centre of the Ecumenical Movement
Globally, young people are turbulent. They are yearning to work, and yet finding themselves on the fringes of society, marginalised and excluded politically and economically. In

some situations, this dismal reality has become fertile ground for religious extremism. The current way of working and the agenda of the church and the ecumenical movement should be radically reshaped to invite young people if we want to revitalise the ecumenical movement, if we want to have fresh visions in unity and mission (Joel 2:28). It is important that we change ourselves to fit into the new generation, rather than asking them to fit into our generation. Transforming ecumenism begins to unfold when young and older people voice their vision of the movement Jesus started and take it forward in their own style. It is time to take radical measures as a most urgent priority with action, budget and staff.

Karlsruhe Assembly: Power of Love to Defeat Fear and Hatred
In the context of the rise of racism and extremism in the world, one of the key goals of the WCC 11th Assembly in Karlsruhe, Germany, in 2022 should be to reflect on how we understand and give expression to the "power of God's love" defeating the culture of hatred and the politics of fear against the other. The power of God's love is superior to the powers of death. We should affirm that the power of the Risen Lord subjugates the powers of death, even as the rest of the world embraces or remains indifferent to the powers of death in God's beloved world. How then can we witness God's love in ways that our witness nurtures, protects and enhances life, while confronting and transforming the denial of God's gift of life? We believe that the gospel has a power to transform the world: personality, value, class, system and society. The gospel of the Kingdom of God challenges the world that keeps nurturing hopelessness. We, as the witnesses of God's love, have a mission to share the Good News with all humanity and creation which are longing for hope.

Ecumenical Discipleship

The Holy Spirit is creating many new hopes with God's people though the ecumenical movement. Our mission is to reveal this hope given to the ecumenical movement to the world through the visible unity of the church and transforming ecumenism. In the midst of agonies, despair and cries of life, it is our mission as ecumenical disciples to recover the One Body of Christ, and to seek alternative values, ways of life and communities to reveal the hope in the Kingdom of God on earth by the power of the Holy Spirit. The ecumenical movement shall be a living witness that the power of love can transform a world of hatred and injustice through our common discipleship.

* **The Rev. Dr. Jooseop Keum** is Distinguished Professor of World Christianity at the Presbyterian University and Theological Seminary, Gwangjin District, Seoul, South Korea. He served the World Council of Churches as director of Commission on World Mission and Evangelism and editor of the *International Review of Mission* from 2007 to 2018. Prior to that, he served the Council for World Mission as executive secretary for mission programme.

Bibliography

Abuom, Agnes. 2018. *Prospects and Challenges for Ecumenism and the Ecumenical Movement, Address to the Swedish Ecumenical Weekend.* https://www.oikoumene.org/en/resources/documents/executive-committee/uppsala-november-2018/prospects-and-challenges-for-ecumenism-and-the-ecumenical-movement.

Agamben, G. 1993. *Coming Community.* Translated by M. Hardt. Minneapolis: University of Minnesota Press.

Angela, Wong Wai Ching. 2004. "Women Doing Theology with the Asian Ecumenical Movement." In *A History of the Ecumenical Movement in Asia.* Vol. 2. Edited by Ninan Koshy. Hong Kong: WSCF AP, YMCA & CCA, 2004.

Anisi, Anna and Aisake Casimira. 2017. "An Historical Overview of Ecumenical Formation and Development." In *Navigating Troubled Waters: The Ecumenical Movement in the Pacific Islands Since the 1980s.* Edited by Manfred Ernst and Lydia Johnson. Suva, Fiji: PTC.

Arai, Tosh and T. K. Thomas. 2002 "Christian Conference of Asia." In *Dictionary of the Ecumenical Movement.* Edited by Nicholas Lossky et al. Second Edition. Geneva: WCC Publications.

Ariarajah, Wesley. 2013. "Ecumenism in Asia as Interfaith Dialogue – A Historical Survey." In *Asian Handbook for Theological Education and Ecumenism.* Edited by Hope Antone et al. Oxford: Regnum Books.

Ariarajah, Wesley. 2016. "The Pioneering Ministry of Stanley J. Samartha," In *A Light to the Nations: The Indian Presence in the Ecumenical Movement in the Twentieth Century.* Edited by Jesudas M. Athyal. Geneva: WCC Publications.

Ariarajah, Wesley. 2017. *Strangers or Co-Pilgrims: The Impact of Interfaith Dialogue on Christian Faith and Practice*. Minneapolis: Fortress Press.

Athyal, Jesudas M. 2017. "The South Asian Presence in the Ecumenical Movement." *The Ecumenical Review* 69/4 (December): 557-569.

Aune, David E. 1997. "Revelation 1-5" In *World Biblical Commentary 52*. Dallas: Word.

Baago, Kaj. 1965. *A History of the National Christian Council of India*. Nagpur: NCCI.

Bühlmann, W. 1977. *The Coming of the Third Church: An Analysis of the Present and Future of the Church*. Maryknoll: Orbis Books.

Burrows, W. R., M. R. Gornik, and J. A. McLean. 2011. *Understanding World Christianity: The Work and Vision of Andrew F. Walls*. Maryknoll: Orbis Books.

Carey, William. "An Enquiry into Obligations of the Christians to Use means for the Conversion of the heathen," in *Classics of Christian Missions*, edited by F. M. DuBose, Nashville: Broadman, 1979.

Carino, Theresa. 2017. "Chinese Churches and the Ecumenical Movement from an Asian Perspective." *The Ecumenical Review* 69/4 (December): 542-556.

Chunakara, Mathew George. 2017. "The Ecumenical Movement in Asia and Emerging Challenges. The Christian Conference of Asia at 60 and Beyond." *The Ecumenical Review* 69/4 (December): 448-461.

Clarke, Sathianathan. 2007. "M. M. Thomas." In *Empire and the Christian Tradition: New Readings of Classical Theologians*. Edited by Kwok Pui-lan, Don H. Compier, and Joerg Rieger. Minneapolis: Fortress Press.

Clarke, Sathianathan. 2014. "World Christianity and Postcolonial Mission: A Path Forward for the Twenty-first Century." *Theology Today*. 71/2: 192-206.

Dharmaraj, Jacob. 1993. Jacob S. *Colonialism and Christian Mission. Postcolonial Reflections*. Delhi: ISPCK.

Duguid-May, Melanie. 2016. "The Ecumenical Movement." In *History of Global Christianity*. Volume III. *History of Christianity in the 20th Century*. Edited by Jens Holger Schjorring, Norman A. Hjelm and Kevin Ward, Leiden, Boston: Brill.

Ecumenical Missionary Conference 1900. 1900. *Report*. Vol. 1. New York: American Tract Society.

Engaging Economic Globalization as a Communion. 2001. Geneva: Lutheran World Federation.

Forman, Charles W. 1986. *The Voice of Many Waters: The Story of the Life and Ministry of the Pacific Conference of Churches in the Last 25 Years.* Suva: Lotu Pasifika Productions.

George, K. M. 2003. "Values for New Ecumenism in Asia." In *Living in Oikoumene.* Edited by Hope S. Antone. Hong Kong: CCA.

Gibran, Kahlil. 2015. "The Madman." In *The Complete Works of Kahlil Gibran.* New Delhi: Cross Land Books.

Gibran, Kahlil. 2015. "The Wanderer." In *The Complete Works of Kahlil Gibran.* New Delhi: Cross Land Books.

Gnanadason, Aruna. 2017. "Asian Women in the Ecumenical Movement. Voices of Resistance and Hope," *The Ecumenical Review* 16/4 (December): 516-526.

Gonzales, Justo L. 2010. *The Story of Christianity.* Vol.1. New York: HarperOne.

Goodall, Norman. Ed. 1968. *The Uppsala Report 1968: Official Report of the Fourth Assembly of the World Council of Churches, Uppsala, July 4-20, 1968.* Geneva: World Council of Churches.

Grant, Robert M. 1975. "Religion and Politics at the Council of Nicaea." *Journal of Religion.* Vol. 55, No. 1 (January): 1-12.

Harding, Vincent. 1969. "Black Power and the American Christ." In *The Black Power Revolt.* Edited by Floyd Barbour. Boston: Beacon Press.

Hau'ofa, Epeli. 1993. "Our Sea of Islands." In *A New Oceania: Rediscovering our Sea of Islands.* Edited by Eric Waddell, Vijay Naidu, and Epeli Hau"ofa. Suva: University of the South Pacific.

Havea, Tevita. 2018. "Uncharted Course in Familiar Waters." Unpublished paper presented at the Pacific Conference of Churches 11th General Assembly, Auckland, New Zealand: October.

Hooft. W. A. Visser't. Ed. 1948. *Man's Disorder and God's Design. 5 vols., vol. 5: The First Assembly of the World Council of Churches, held at Amsterdam, August 22nd to September 4th, 1948.* The Amsterdam Assembly Series. New York: Harper & Brothers.

Howard-Brook, Wes. 2016. *Empire Baptized. How the Church Embraced What Jesus Rejected* (Second-Fifth Centuries), Maryknoll, New York: Orbis Books.

Irvin, D.T. 2008. "World Christianity: An Introduction." *The Journal of World Christianity*. 1/1.

Jenkins, Philip. 2002. *The Next Christendom. The Coming of Global Christianity.* New York: Oxford University Press.

Joseph, M. P. 2007. "Revisiting the Edinburgh Conference in the Context of Globalization." In *Witnessing in Context. Essays in Honor of Eardly Mendis.* Edited by Monica J. Melanchthon and George Zachariah. Tiruvalla:CSS.

Kang, Namsoon. 2010. "Whose/Which World in World Christianity?: Toward World Christianity as Christianity of Worldly-Responsibility." In *A New Day: Essays on World Christianity in Honor of Lamin Sanneh.* Edited by Andrew F. Walls and Akintunde E. Akinade. New York: Peter Lang.

Kappen, Sebastian. 1995. *Spirituality in the Age of Reconciliation.* Bangalore: Visthar.

Kasdorf, H. 1990. *Gustav Warnecks Missiologisches Erbe. Eine Biographisch-historische Untersuchung.* Gießen und Basel: Brunnen Verlag.

Katoppo, Marianne. 1980. *Compassionate and Free: An Asian Woman's Theology.* Maryknoll, New York: Orbis.

Kinnamon, Michael. Ed. 1991. *Sings of the Spirit: Official Report Seventh Assembly, Canberra, Australia, 7-20 February 1991.* Geneva: World Council of Churches.

Kollman, P. V. 2014. "Understanding the World-Christian Turn in the History of Christianity and Theology." *Theology Today.* 71/2: 164–177.

Koschorke, Klaus. 2014. "New Maps of the History of World Christianity: Current Challenges and Future Perspectives." *Theology Today.* 71/2: 178-191.

Kyo-Seong, Ahn. 2013. "The Asian Context and the Ecumenical Movement of the Korean Church." *Korean Presbyterian Journal of Theology* 45/3 (2013): 37-61.

Kyung, Chung Hyun. 1990. *Struggle to be the Sun Again. Introducing Asian Women's Theology.* Maryknoll, NY: Orbis.

Lisak, Marcin. 2016. "Socio-Religious Perspectives on the Ecumenical Paradigm Shift according to Konrad Raiser and Hans Kueng." *Angelicum* 93: 109-133.

Longchar, Wati. 2007. "Ecumenical Movement in Asia: Can we Make a Difference?" *CTC Bulletin* 23/3 (August): 109-114. Retrieved from:

https://www.cca.org.hk/ctc/ctc07-02/12_wati_longchar109.pdf

MacCulloch, Diarmaid. 2009. *A History of Christianity. The First Three Thousand Years,* New York:Viking.

Mamak, Alexander and Grant McCall. Eds. 1978. *Paradise Postponed: Essays on Research and Development in the South Pacific.* Rushcutters Bay, AU: Pergamon Press.

Manchala, Deenabandhu. 2011. "Expanding the Ambit: Dalit Theological Contribution to Ecumenical Social Thought." In *Dalit Theology in the Twenty-first Century: Discordant Voices, Discerning Pathways.* Edited by Sathianathan Clarke, Deenabandhu Manchala, and Philip Vinod Peacock. New Delhi: Oxford University Press.

Mott, John R. 1900. *The Evangelization of the World in This Generation.* New York: Student Volunteer Movement for Foreign Missions.

Mott, John R. 1979. "The Obligation to Evangelize the World." Reprinted in *Classics of Christian Missions.* Edited by F. M. DuBose, Nashville: Broadman.

Melanchthon, Monica. 2007. "The Editorial: The Haunts of Pain: Theologizing Dalits." *In God's Image* 26:3 (September): 1-8.

Myers, Bruce. 2013. "Keeping Warm. Reception in the Ecumenical Winter." *The Ecumenical Review* 65/3 (October): 376-387.

Nagy, D. 2010. "Where Is China in World Christianity?" *Diversities.* 12/1: 70–83.

New Delhi Statement on Unity and Orthodox Response. 1961. Retrieved from: www.wcc-coe.org/wcc/who/crete-o2-e.html

Newbigin, Leslie. 1986. *Foolishness to the Greeks: Gospel and Western Culture.* Grand Rapids, MI: Eerdmans.

Newbigin, Leslie. 1989. *The Gospel in a Pluralist Society.* Geneva: WCC.

Newbigin, Leslie. 1991. *Truth to Tell: The Gospel as Public Truth.* Grand Rapids, MI: Eerdmans.

Newbigin, Leslie. 1995. *The Open Secret: An Introduction to the Theology of Mission.* Grand Rapids, MI: Eerdmans.

Nicolet, Claude. 1991. *Space, Geography, and Politics in the Early Roman Empire.* Ann Arbor: University of Michigan Press.

Nokise, Fele. 2011. "Ecumenism and its Hermeneutical Experience in Oceania." *The Pacific Journal of Theology* Series II, No. 46: 95-127.

Oommen, George. 2015. "Challenging Identity and Crossing Borders: Unity in the Church of South India." *Word & World* 25/1.

ÖRK-Chef: Wir leben im ökumenischen Winter. 2010. Radio Vatican. December 5.

Pacific Church Leaders Meeting. 2017. "Sowing a New Seed of Pacific Ecumenism". Unpublished Statement of Basis and Resolution issued in Nadi, 12 October.

Pacific Conference of Churches. 2010. "Rethinking the Household of God in the Pacific: Concept Paper for Church Leaders," 2010, http://www. actnowpng.org/sites/default/files/Re-thinking%20Oceania%20pc.pdf

Patta, Raj Bharat. 2016. "'Lengthen Thy Cords and Strengthen Thy Stakes': Augustine Ralla Ram's Ecumenical Missional Contributions." In *A Light to the Nations. The Indian Presence in the Ecumenical Movement in the Twentieth Century.* Edited by Jesudas M. Athyal. Geneva: World Council of Churches.

Pelikan, Jaroslav. 1987. *The Excellent Empire: The Fall of Rome and the Triumph of the Church.* San Francisco: Harper & Row.

Perera, Marlene. 1995. "New Models and New Praxis." In *Women's Visions.* Edited by Ofelia Ortega. Geneva: WCC.

Phan, Peter C. 2007. "Christian Social Spirituality: A Global Perspective." In *Catholic Social Justice: Theological and Practical Explorations.* Edited by Philomena Cullen, Bernard Hoose, and Gerard Mannion. New York: Continuum.

Philip, T. V. 1994. *Ecumenism in Asia.* Delhi: ISPCK & CSS.

Policy Reference Committee II, Report 8.4, Appendix II: Globalization, In *Together on the Way: The Harare Report.* Edited by D. Kessler. Geneva: World Council of Churches. 1998.

Polybius. (n.d). *Histories* 3.1.4.

Pui-lan, Kwok. 2000. *Introducing Asian Feminist Theology.* Sheffield: Sheffield Academic Press, 2000.

Raiser, Konrad. 1991. *Ecumenism in Transition.* Geneva: WCC.

Raiser, Konrad. 1997. "Ecumenism in Search of a New Vision." In *The Ecumenical Movement: An Anthology of Key Texts and Voices.* Edited by Michael Kinnamon and Brian E. Cope. Geneva: WCC/Grand Rapids: Eerdmans.

Raiser, Konrad. 1997. *To be the Church.* Geneva: WCC.

Raiser, Konrad. 2002. *Dictionary of the Ecumenical Movement.* Edited by Nicholas Lossky et. al. Geneva: WCC.

Ralla Ram, Augustine. 1956. "Organic Church Unity: A Comment From India." *The Ecumenical Review* 8/3 (April): 243-248.

Report of the General Secretary. 2002. *Ecumenical Review* 54:4 (October): 501-502.

Richard, Pablo. 1995. *Apocalypse: A People's Commentary on the Book of Revelation,* Maryknoll, NY: Orbis.

Root, Michael. 2018. "Ecumenical Winter" http://www.firstthings.com/article/2018/10/ecumenicalwinter

Rossing, Barbara R. 2002. "'Alas for the Earth!' Lament and Resistance in Revelation 12." In *The Earth Bible. Vol. 5: The Earth Story in the New Testament.* Edited by Norman Habel and Shirley Wurth. Sheffield: Sheffield Academic Press.

Rossing, Barbara R. 2003. "(Re)claiming *Oikoumene?* Empire, Ecumenism, and the Discipleship of Equals." In *Walk in the Ways of Wisdom: Essays in Honor of Elisabeth Schuessler Fiorenza.* Edited by Shelly Matthews et. al. Harrisburg/London/New York: Trinity Press International.

Said, Edward. 1978. *Orientalism.* London: Pantheon Books. Reprint: 1995.

Sanecki, Kim Caroline. 2016. "Protestant Christian Missions, Race and Empire: The World Missionary Conference of 1910, Edinburgh, Scotland." Doctoral Dissertation submitted to the Department of History of the Georgia State University. Retrieved from: https://scholarworks.gsu.edu/history_theses/10.

Sanneh, Lamin. 2003. *Whose Religion is Christianity? The Gospel beyond the West.* Grand Rapids and Cambridge: William B. Eerdmans Publishing Company.

Sawyerr, H. 1978. "The First World Missionary Conference. Edinburgh 1910." *International Review of Mission,* LXVII (1978): 255–272.

Spivak, Gayatri C. 2000. "Can the Subaltern Speak?," In *Postcolonialism. Critical Concepts.* Edited by D. Brydon. Vol. IV. London and New York: Routledge.

Talapusi, Faitala. 1994. "The Future of Theology in the Pacific." Paper Presented at the EATWOT Conference, Suva, Fiji, September 14.

Thoma, Juhanon Mar. 2011. *Christianity in India and a Brief History of the Mar Thoma Church*. Tiruvalla: CSS.

Thomas, Larry. 2006. "Vaka Vuku: Navigating Knowledge." Paper presented at Pacific Epistemologies Conference. University of the South Pacific, Suva, Fiji, July 3-7.

Thomas, M.M. 1976. "The Cross and the Kingdom of God," In *New Creation in Christ*. Delhi: ISPCK.

Thomas, M. M. 1983. *Ideological Quest within Christian Commitment*. Bangalore/Madras: CISRS/CLS.

Thomas, M. M. 1988. "An Assessment of Tambaram's Contribution to the Search of the Asian Churches for an Authentic Selfhood." *International Review of Mission*. 77/307 (July): 390-397.

Thomas, M. M. and P. T. Thomas. 1992. *Towards an Indian Christian Theology*. Tiruvalla: CLS.

Tui Atua Tupua Tamasese Ta'isi Efi. 2014. "Whispers and Vanities in Samoan Indigenous Religious Culture." In *Whispers and Vanities: Samoan Indigenous Knowledge and Religion*. Edited by Tamasailau M. Suaalii-Sauni et.al. Wellington: New Zealand Huia Publishers.

Vinayaraj, Y.T. 2010. "Re-visiting 'the other': Towards a postmodern understanding of Christian mission." Retrieved from http://revytvinayaraj.blogspot.com/p/theology.html

Vinayaraj, Y.T. 2013. "Reconfiguring 'Christian Unity': Towards an Ecumenism of 'Manyness.'" *Bangalore Theological Forum*. Vol. XLV, No. 2 (December): 116-125.

Walls, Andrew F. and A. E. Akinade. 2010. *A New Day: Essays on World Christianity in Honor of Lamin Sanneh*. New York: Peter Lang, 2010

Wicks, Jared. 2018. *Investigating Vatican II: Its Theologians, Ecumenical Turn, and Biblical Commitment*. Washingdon, DC: Catholic University of America Press.

World Missionary Conference 1910. n.d. *The History and Records of the Conference Together with Addresses Delivered at the Evening Meetings*. Edinburgh: Oliphant, Anderson & Ferrier.

World Missionary Conference 1910. 1910. *Report of Commission I: Carrying the Gospel to all the Non-Christian World*. Edinburgh and London: Oliphant, Anderson & Ferrier; New York, Chicago and Toronto: Fleming H. Revell Company.

World Missionary Conference. 1991. *One World*. March-April.

Yong-Bok, K. 2004. "Asian Quest for Jesus in Global Empire." *Madang*. 1/2.

Zachariah, George. 2016. "Poulose Mar Poulose: An Activist of Alternative Ecumenism." In *A Light to the Nations. The Indian Presence in the Ecumenical Movement in the Twentieth Century*. Edited by Jesudas M. Athyal. Geneva: World Council of Churches.